A Mind for Math
Level D

Genesis Curriculum
The Book of Genesis

First Edition

Welcome to *A Mind for Math*, the level D workbook. This workbook gives you a place for your daily work. You'll work through the lesson with your parent/teacher, listening and answering questions. You'll be doing each level of the lessons. This workbook will give you a place to write your answers and do your work.

It's good to learn to work the numbers in your head and use mental math, but it's also a good habit to write down work, as well as the answers. Math will get more and more involved, and you won't always be able to do it in your head. Maybe on the first levels you can try to answer the questions in your head and just write down your answer, and then write the work out for the last level.

Most lessons are on one page, but some will continue onto a second page. Don't miss it when it does.

Make sure to listen to the lessons and not just work ahead. In the lessons there will be more directions, more questions, and even hints for you.

Hope you have a great year. I hope that you'll find math fun and exciting.

Day 1

Add 12 hours for morning and 12 hours for evening together to see if you get one full day.

There was morning and evening, one day. If there had been morning, evening, and morning again, how long would that have been?

If there had been two full days, how long would that have been?

If there had been two "mornings" and two "evenings," how long would that have been?

Now add on another half a day.

Does 12 + 12 = 24?   Let's do that with two full days, 24 + 24.

What is forty plus eight?

Now, let's add two days and another half a day. How many hours do we need to add together?

Find the total number of hours in four days. That's the hours of two days plus the hours of two days.

<u>Tens   Ones</u>   <u>Tens   Ones</u>

Find the total number of hours of:

6 days   24 x 6 = 20 x 6 and 20 x 4 =

7 days

8 days

9 days

Day 2

Which day comes after the second day?   Which day comes two before the fourth day?

Which day comes five after the third day?   Which day comes three before the tenth day?

Identify each number below as odd or even. (Write O or E under each.)

24   36   81   247   eighteenth   twelfth   fifteenth   100

Multiply five by:

14

17

19

26

Multiply.

53 x 9

28 x 7

86 x 5

49 x 7

Day 3

How many seeds did two apples produce if they produced 6 seeds? 7 seeds? 8 seeds? 9 seeds? 10 seeds?

Figure out how many seeds there would be if you had three apples and each had 1 seed. Then figure it out for 2 seeds, 3 seeds, 4 seeds, and 5 seeds. Skip count by threes.

What do you think happens when you quadruple or quintuple numbers? That's multiplying them by 4 or 5. Check to see if you are correct.

Is 123 x 256 an odd or even number?

Is 4,939 x 5,800 an odd or even number?

Multiply these numbers to check it out.

    13 x 9   18 x 7

    16 x 4   19 x 6

Multiply. You can do a basic check of your answer by seeing if it's odd or even.

    73 x 8

    92 x 4

    45 x 6

    85 x 7

Day 4

Write one, ten, and one hundred on the chart below. Write two, twenty, and two hundred on the chart.

<u>Hundreds Tens Ones</u>

Write these numbers in the place value chart. 789   521   2,047   1,839
    Circle the greatest number.

<u>Thousands Hundreds Tens Ones</u>

Write these numbers in the place value chart. 5,421   20,647   18,309
    Circle the greatest number.

<u>Ten Thousand Thousands Hundreds Tens Ones</u>

Write these numbers in the place value chart. 35,401   209,087   1,128,006
    Circle the greatest number.

<u>Million   Hundred Thousand Ten Thousand Thousands Hundreds Tens Ones</u>

Day 5
Review

How many hours are in five days?

How many hours are in ten days?

How many hours are in eleven days?

Multiply.

   78 x 9

   35 x 4

   83 x 6

   92 x 8

Write these numbers in the place value chart. 5,051   49,846   2,017,403

<u>Million Hundred Thousand Ten Thousand Thousands Hundreds Tens Ones</u>

Day 6

5 x 2 =	5 x 3 =	5 x 4 =	5 x 5 =
5 x 6 =	5 x 7 =	5 x 8 =	4 x 0 =
4 x 1 =	4 x 2 =	4 x 3 =	4 x 4 =
4 x 5 =	4 x 6 =	4 x 7 =	4 x 8 =
5 x 6 =	4 x 7 =	3 x 9 =	8 x 8 =
7 x 6 =	9 x 5 =	10 x 3 =	11 x 4 =

12 x 6 =

13 x 8 =

14 x 7 =

15 x 9 =

64 x 7 =

82 x 9 =

75 x 6 =

48 x 8 =

Day 7

What is double one million?

Double these numbers: 7   8   9   10   100   400

Double these numbers: 14   32   50   241   430

```
  241
 +241
_____
```

Double these numbers: 75, 98, 26, 48, 219. Add the hundreds. Add the tens. Add the ones. Put them all together.

75   98   26

48   219

Double these numbers:

1218

2393

450

392

Day 8

Draw one line through each shape to divide it in half.

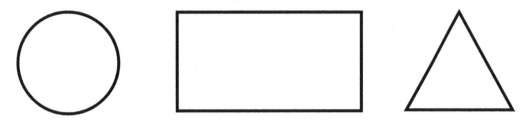

Draw another line on all those shapes to divide them in half another way.

Draw as many lines of symmetry as you can for a square.

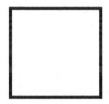

Shapes can have multiple, or many, lines of symmetry. How many lines of symmetry does the triangle have?

the rectangle?   the circle?

Draw a shape with only one line of symmetry and one shape with none.

Day 9

Count up objects in an area and as you count, make tally marks. Draw a line for each thing you count. |||| That shows you counted four things. When you get to five, you draw a line diagonally across the whole group.

Count these lines with no tricks, just straight counting. Write down your answer.

Then use tally marks to bundle them into fives. Then you might want to divide them into groups of twenty or however else you find useful and then count them up.

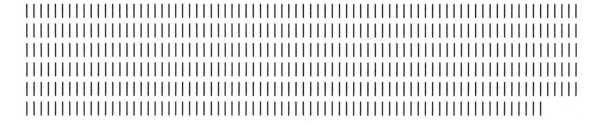

Count up all the money you can find in the house. First organize it; sorting can help your counting. Put each separate denomination of bill and coin in its own pile. Then put the coins into piles of one dollar. Then you can easily go through and count up the dollars and then just add on any remaining cents.

Day 10
Review

Multiply.

58 x 9

26 x 7

73 x 8

83 x 4

Double these numbers:

1427   384   2050   293

Draw a shape with only one line of symmetry and one with none.

If you need the practice, count up all the money you can find in the house. First organize it; sorting can help your counting. Put each separate denomination of bill and coin in its own pile. Then put the coins into piles of one dollar. Then you can easily go through and count up the dollars and then just add on any remaining cents.

If you like, you can make a shape with one line of symmetry by folding a piece of paper in half and cutting out a design, while leaving the fold intact. When you open the paper, the fold will be the line of symmetry.

Day 11

Double these numbers and read your answers out loud:

4   40   400   6   60   600   8   80   800

There are 140 plants and 70 are removed. How many are left?

Try it with these numbers and read your answers out loud:

$90 - 40$ $160 - 70$ $140 - 80$

$1100 - 300$ $800 + 900$

300 times 50 = 3 x 5 with three zeros = 15,000

Try this. How many pieces of fruit are in an orchard if there are 80 trees and each tree has 50 pieces of fruit?

Now try with these numbers and then read your answers out loud.

400 x 80

700 x 900

120 x 400

500 x 60

Divide one million by ten six times. What's the answer the last time?

$1,000,000 \div 10 =$

$100,000 \div 10 =$

$10,000 \div 10 =$

$1,000 \div 10 =$

$100 \div 10 =$

$10 \div 10 =$

Break apart these numbers like this $20 = 2 \times 10$.

40

90

500

Try it with these numbers and read your answers out loud.

$320 \div 40$

$630 \div 90$

$1000 \div 100$

$2000 \div 500$

Day 12

```
     tens | ones
       4  |  1
       3  |  6
```

Now to expand numbers we break them up into tens and ones like this:

36 is 30 and 6.
We write 30 + 6.

Expand 23, 56 and 81 in the same way. Turn them into addition problems that separate the tens and ones.

23   56   81

You can expand numbers with hundreds in the same way.

287 is 200 + 80 + 7 in expanded form, as we call it.

Expand.

517

628

349

Expand these numbers: 2571, 1080, 9804, and 6736. Write them in expanded form.

2571

1080

9804

6736

What is this number in standard form (just as a normal number)?

5000 + 700 + 20 + 3

Write these numbers in expanded form: 10,507 ; 26,784 ; 58,001.

10,507

26,784

58,001

What is this number in standard form?

70,000 + 9000 + 800 + 40 + 6

Day 13

Draw a line. Pretend that's a river. Draw a line to divide it in half, split it in two. Here's the number one half. ½

If each side were a river, where could you draw two more lines to divide each of those rivers in half? Draw the lines. How many pieces of river do you have now?

Let's work with another shape. Draw a circle.

Divide the circle lake into four quarters by drawing a line to divide it in half and then another line to divide it in half the other way. Color in one half of the circle. How many fourths is that?

Draw one more circle next to it and color in one quarter of it. When one quarter is colored in, how many fourths of that circle are not colored in?

Here is how you write one fourth. ¼   How do you write three fourths?

Draw another circle above and pretend it's a lake. Color in one third of it. How many parts of the lake aren't colored in? How would you write that as a fraction?

Write one half and one fourth as fractions. How many quarters is one half?

Add one half and one fourth. Draw the answer. Color in two fourths (one half) and one more fourth. How many fourths are colored in?

Write the fractions and answer as an equation such as 2 + 1 = 3.

Day 14

If there were 16 trees in the garden and the man were allowed to eat from them all except 8, how many trees was he allowed to eat from?

Now try with these numbers: 13 trees except 7, 14 trees except 5, 12 trees except 9

If there were 64 trees in the garden, and he were allowed to eat from all except 20, how many trees was he allowed to eat from?

Now try with these numbers: 55 trees except 13, 76 trees except 24, 90 trees except 40.

If there were 34 trees and he were allowed to eat from all of them except 25, how many trees was he allowed to eat from?

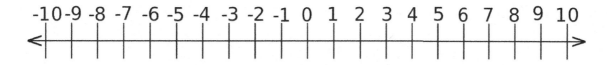

Try it with these numbers: 35 trees except 26, 41 trees except 35, 62 trees except 53

If he were allowed to eat from 82 trees except for 58 of them, how many were he allowed to eat from?

Now try it with these numbers: 93 trees except 38, 84 trees except 67, 75 trees except 49

Day 15
Review

Multiply and divide. 480 ÷ 60, 720 ÷ 90, 800 ÷ 100, 4000 ÷ 500

Write these numbers in expanded form: 19,537 and 8,001.

What is this number in standard form?

80,000 + 4,000 +200 + 10 + 5

Add together one third and one sixth. This is just like adding one half and one fourth. Follow the same thought process and pattern.

If he were allowed to eat from 72 trees except for 58 of them, how many was he allowed to eat from?

Now try it with these numbers: 82 trees except 39, 73 trees except 67, 64 trees except 49

Day 16

Adam had 24 ribs and God took away one. How many did he have left?

Practice subtraction by finding the differences between the number below and then make up a word problem about taking away for you parent to answer. You do it too so you can check if the answer is correct!

17	15	12	13	15	16
- 9	- 8	- 7	- 6	- 7	- 9

19	27	25	35	29	48
- 11	- 13	- 25	- 23	- 18	- 38

21	273	784	85	291
- 6	- 55	- 270	- 36	- 174

659	540	348	630
- 412	- 235	- 285	- 144

Day 17

Design a garden. Draw it out. Place your orchard. Draw a fence around it to keep out unwanted animals who would eat your fruit.

When you are done, measure around your garden. Measure each side to the nearest centimeter. A parent or older sibling can help you if you aren't sure how to measure. Write down the measurement of each side and then add them all together. That is the perimeter of your garden.

Then find the "real" measurement of your garden. Let's say that each centimeter is 6 feet in real life.

> 1 centimeter on your drawing = 6 x 1 feet in real life

Day 18

There are patterns in today's reading. There's a pattern of behavior in Adam and Eve both blaming others for their sin. There's a pattern in God cursing each in turn, the serpent, the woman, and the man.

Today you are going to make patterns. A pattern is a repetition. You could repeat shapes, number, actions, rhythms.

An example of a shape pattern would be to draw a line, a circle, and a star, and then repeat it.

Everyone is going to make patterns for others to carry on. Find the pattern and continue it.

An example of a word pattern would be words that each start with the next letter of the alphabet: apple, bear, candle, dog, etc.

An example of a mathematical pattern would be to add five to each number like this: 1 6 11 16 21, etc.

A harder pattern involves more mathematical figuring on each number.   0, 1, 6, 31, 156

Day 19

Look at this diagram. Picture the sword stationed at the letter B and it turning and putting its point at A, D, and C.

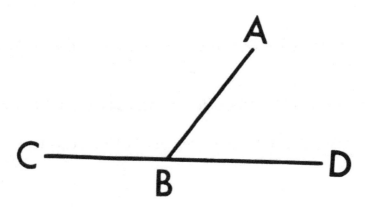

Draw 360 degrees on our ABCD picture.

Now what would be the measure of a half circle?

That would be the measure from where to where on our ABCD picture?

Lines have the angle measure of 180°. That's how we write degrees.

The three inner angles made at each point add up to 180. If the sides are all the same length, the angles are the same length. What's the angle?

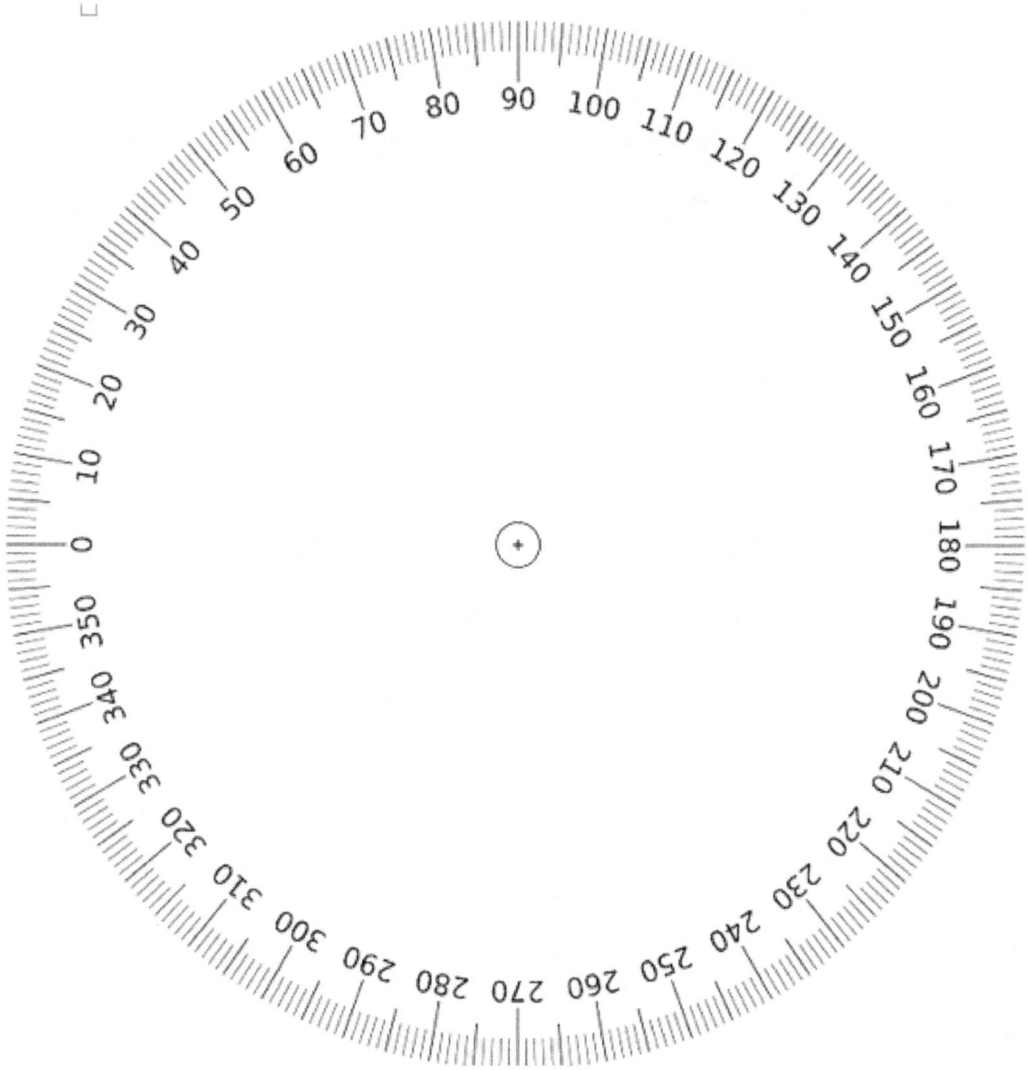
0
10
20
30
40
50
60
70
80
90
100
110
120
130
140
150
160
170
180
190
200
210
220
230
240
250
260
270
280
290
300
310
320
330
340
350

Day 20
Review

659	540	348	630
- 412	- 235	- 285	- 144

Take these four numbers as measure of sides of a shape. Find the perimeter.

659   540   348   630

Multiply 47 x 8.

What is the pattern? What is the next number? Bonus: What number comes after that?

1, 2, 6, 24, 120

A triangle's angles always add up to 180 degrees. If two of the angles are 45 degrees, what is the measure of the third angle?

Day 21

What hour would you read on these clocks?

What time does this clock say?

Read these clocks.

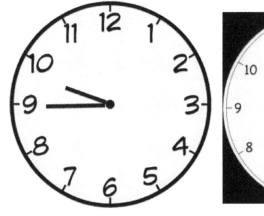  

Read these clocks to the nearest minute. The extra line there that's thinner than the others is the second hand.

Day 22

Multiply 7 by 1, 2, 3, 5, and 10. Use skip counting. Use the chart to help you.

Multiplying is adding. Multiplying 1 x 7 = 1 + 1 + 1 + 1 + 1 + 1 +1. Add 2 + 2 + 2 + 2 + 2 + 2 + 2 and see if you get the same answer as when you multiplied and used skip counting.

Add fourteen to twenty-five. Write fourteen on the chart to show those answers.

tens	ones		tens	ones		tens	ones		tens	ones		tens	ones
2	5												

What if you were to add thirty-five to twenty-three or sixty-one to twenty-three?

What is 49, seven times? Do it by adding and then by multiplying.

What is 68, seven times? Do it by adding and then by multiplying.

Now what's 343 and 476 seven times? Do each by adding and then by multiplying.

Day 23

Draw four lines. Let's pretend Cain had four sons. If he built a city for half of them, how many had cities built for them? Circle half of the lines.

Redraw your four lines so that there are two together and then the other two together. Circle one in each pair.

If there were six sons and half of them had a city, how many had a city? Draw a picture to match your answer. Then write the fraction one half. It's the number one over the number two with a little line between them.

If a quarter of his sons had a city and he had eight sons, how many had cities? A quarter is one fourth, one out of every four. Draw a picture to show that. Find four and circle one of those. Then find another four.

Find one fourth of twelve sons and sixteen sons.

Can you find the pattern? If a quarter of his sons had a city and 5 sons had cities, how many sons did he have?

Find one third of 15 sons. Find two thirds of 21 sons. Label your answers.

Find one third of 21. ($^1/_3$) 21 is one way to write that. That means one third times twelve. That means 21 x 1, which is 21 and divided by 3, which is what?

What do you think is ($^2/_3$) 21?

($^1/_3$) 27 =   ($^2/_3$) 27 =

(¼) 36 =   (¾) 24 =

Day 24

Put the symbol between the numbers below to show which is smaller and which is bigger.

23   51   102   78   124   160

Write which is the biggest.   17 + 14 or 28 + 5

Now try with these numbers.

1097   3012   230   200 + 15 + 17

What's greater 72 x 7 or 59 x 8?

Now try it with these numbers:

21,451   20,989   9 x 62   5 x 71

27 x 72 or 34 x 58 Compare their answers using a greater than/less than symbol.

Try one more time. Which is bigger? 17 x 46 or 29 x 35

Day 25
Review

What time does the clock say?

$(^1/_3)$ 18 =

$(^4/_5)$ 30 =

(¾) 36 =

$(^3/_8)$ 40 =

Which is greater? 26 x 54 or 31 x 47

Which is bigger? 18 x 23 or 15 x 34

Day 26
Review

159	149	234	860
+ 412	+ 235	+ 348	+ 140

What time is it?

How many hours is 32 days?

Which is bigger? 26 x 17 or 24 x 19

Day 27
Review

155	143	231	580
+ 482	+ 275	+ 398	+ 420

What time does the clock say?

Draw a shape with only one line of symmetry.

Find the sum: 170 + 103 + 256 + 369

Multiply. 75 x 6

Double 1465.

Day 28

$$219 + 412$$ $$182 + 255$$ $$296 + 348$$ $$373 + 148$$

Write fifty-six thousand two hundred fifty-nine on the chart.

ten thousands	thousands	hundreds	tens	ones

Write this number in expanded form: 43,085.

Divide. 2000 ÷ 400

What is 4000 + 30 + 7 number in standard form?

$(^3/_5)$ 30 = $(^4/_7)$ 49 =

Day 29
Review

259	586	265	367
+ 464	+ 235	+ 348	+ 347

These are inch measurements of the sides of a shape. Find the perimeter. 422, 260, 325, 25

Multiply: 53 x 700

What would the area be of a rectangle width of 7 cm. and a length of 34 cm.?

Day 30
Review

$56 \div 7 =$ $81 \div 9 =$ $64 \div 8 =$ $24 \div 3 =$

$42 \div 6 =$ $45 \div 9 =$ $36 \div 6 =$ $49 \div 7 =$

$30 \div 5 =$ $32 \div 8 =$ $28 \div 4 =$ $21 \div 7 =$

$$\begin{array}{r} 67 \\ \times\ 8 \\ \hline \end{array} \qquad \begin{array}{r} 26 \\ \times\ 4 \\ \hline \end{array} \qquad \begin{array}{r} 39 \\ \times\ 9 \\ \hline \end{array} \qquad \begin{array}{r} 45 \\ \times\ 700 \\ \hline \end{array}$$

$$\begin{array}{r} 45 \\ \times 18 \\ \hline \end{array} \qquad \begin{array}{r} 42 \\ \times 26 \\ \hline \end{array} \qquad \begin{array}{r} 39 \\ \times 47 \\ \hline \end{array} \qquad \begin{array}{r} 28 \\ \times\ 57 \\ \hline \end{array}$$

$180 \div 3 =$ $90 \div 3 =$

Day 31
Review

```
  659          540          890          630
- 412        - 235        - 308        - 144
```

Multiply.

38 x 9   72 x 41

Write this number on the place value chart. 6,802,143

Million   Hundred Thousand Ten Thousand Thousands Hundreds Tens Ones

Which is bigger? 1879 + 2395 or 15 x 34

Day 32
Review

```
  672          543          564          500
- 482        - 275        - 398        - 420
```

What's double this number? 762

Draw a shape with no lines of symmetry.

Which is greater? 62 x 45 or 34 x 74

Day 33
Review

$$412 - 211 \qquad 282 - 255 \qquad 426 - 348 \qquad 373 - 148$$

How many lines of symmetry does a rectangle have?

Add together two thirds and one sixth.

If he were allowed to eat from 84 trees except for 27 of them, how many was he allowed to eat from?

(¾) 48 =   ($^5/_8$) 56 =

Day 34
Review

451	586	365	345
- 264	- 235	- 348	- 317

Multiply: 64 x 300

Find the sum: 689 + 129 + 387

What would the area be of a rectangle width of 15 centimeters and a length of 29 cm?

Day 35
Review

63 ÷ 7 =   36 ÷ 9 =   56 ÷ 8 =   27 ÷ 3 =

24 ÷ 6 =   54 ÷ 9 =   42 ÷ 6 =   35 ÷ 7 =

40 ÷ 5 =   48 ÷ 8 =   32 ÷ 4 =   28 ÷ 7 =

$$
\begin{array}{r} 45 \\ \times\ 6 \\ \hline \end{array}
\qquad
\begin{array}{r} 37 \\ \times\ 8 \\ \hline \end{array}
\qquad
\begin{array}{r} 24 \\ \times\ 7 \\ \hline \end{array}
\qquad
\begin{array}{r} 89 \\ \times\ 4 \\ \hline \end{array}
$$

$$
\begin{array}{r} 17 \\ \times\ 28 \\ \hline \end{array}
\qquad
\begin{array}{r} 31 \\ \times\ 76 \\ \hline \end{array}
\qquad
\begin{array}{r} 58 \\ \times\ 55 \\ \hline \end{array}
\qquad
\begin{array}{r} 29 \\ \times\ 47 \\ \hline \end{array}
$$

475 ÷ 5 =   840 ÷ 5 =

Day 36

1 x 2 = 2   2 x 2 =   2 x   =   2 x   =

Can you do it one more time?

Here's the first one 1 + 1 = 2. Now keep going until you get to 64. Then how would you add 64 and 64?

Let's multiply by each of your previous answers: 2, 4, 8, 16, 32, 64, 128. Multiply them by 1, 2, 3, 4, 5, 6, and 7 respectively. (2 x 1, 4 x 2, 8 x 3, etc.)

Take all the answers you just found and do the same thing! (2 x 1, 8 x 2, 24 x 3, etc.)

Day 37

Figure out what goes in the blanks.

$8 +$ _____ $= 15$ $8 +$ _____ $= 14$ $8 +$ _____ $= 17$

$10 +$ _____ $= 15$ $20 +$ _____ $= 40$ $52 +$ _____ $= 75$

$45 +$ _____ $= 60$ $14 +$ _____ $= 22$ _____ $- 5 = 30$
                                                              Pay attention!

_____ $- 23 = 70$ $5 \times$ _____ $= 75$
                                                Think! Try!

$385 +$ _____ $= 392$ $154 +$ _____ $= 221$

_____ $\times 11 = 132$ $5 \times$ _____ $= 150$
Think! Try!

_____ $\div 7 = 728$ _____ $\div 8 = 320$

Day 38

God gave Noah measurements for the ark: 300 cubits long, 50 cubits wide, 30 cubits high.

Find the perimeter in centimeters. Add up all the sides. How will you add 50 and 50? Look at how you can add 30 + 30.

$$
\begin{array}{r} 30 \\ + \ 30 \\ \hline 0 \end{array}
\qquad
\begin{array}{r} 50 \\ + \ 50 \\ \hline \end{array}
\qquad
\begin{array}{r} 300 \\ + \ 300 \\ \hline \end{array}
$$

Now, let's say that every 10 cubits is one inch. You would measure that by measuring 30 inches long and 5 inches wide. Measure that and mark it off.

Find the perimeter in inches.

Find the area for centimeters and inches, using the numbers above. Area is length times width. 10 x 10 is just 1 x 1 with two zeros tagged onto the end. 30 x 100 is 3 x 1 with two zeros tagged onto the end.

300 x 50 =

30 x 5 =

To find the volume of the boat, you multiply the length times the width times the height. Find the volume in inches and centimeters cubed.

Now let's say that every 5 cubits is a centimeter. To find what measurements we need, we can divide.

Groups	Total	
	715	You can write it on a chart like this.
	715	Number of toys
100	- 500	Take out 100 groups of 5, 5 x 100 = 500
	215	Find out how many toys are left
40	- 200	We've taken out 40 groups (boxes) with is 200 toys (40 x 5).
	15	There are twelve toys left in the barrel.
3	- 15	We can take out three boxes. 3 x 4 = 12
143	0	We took out 23 boxes and there are no toys left in the barrel.

Groups	Total
	715
100	- 500
	215
10	- 50
	165
10	- 50
	115
10	- 50
	65
10	- 50
	15
1	- 5
	10
1	- 5
	5
1	- 5
143	0

Here it is if you aren't sure how many you can take out.

So, to find our numbers we'd find 300 ÷ 5 , 50 ÷ 5, and 30 ÷ 5.

You should know 30 and 50 divided by 5. Divide 300 by five to find the number of centimeters the scale model would be if every 5 cubits were 1 centimeter.

Width =

Height =

Length =

Day 39

If seven of every clean animal entered the ark and two of every unclean animal, how many animals were there if there were three types clean animals and three types of unclean animals?

How many animals were there if there were just two types of the unclean and two types of the clean?

How many animals were there if there were five types of unclean animals and two types of clean animals?

Now figure out how many animals were on the ark if there were 5 types of each clean and unclean animals.

Try it with these numbers: 8 types of each, 4 types of each, 6 types of each.

Try it with these numbers: 12 types of each, 25 types of each, 37 types of each.

Try it with these numbers: 89 types of each, 100 types of each, 107 types of each.

Day 40
Review

_____ x 6 = 168　　　　　5 x _____ = 235

_____ ÷ 4 = 378　　　　　_____ ÷ 8 = 165

_____ x 7 = 98　　　　　6 x _____ = 204

_____ ÷ 7 = 215　　　　　_____ ÷ 4 = 268

205 x 6 =　　**1230**　　　　37 x 8 = **296**

Day 41

How many days does July, August, September, and October have all together?

How many minutes are in a day?

How many minutes are in a week?

Let's divide by four and see if these years are leap years.

Let's solve 2016 ÷ 4 = 504. If we can divide a year by 4 and there are no "years" left in the barrel, then it is a leap year.

Groups	Total
	2016
500	- 2000
	16
4	- 16
504	0

5 x 4 = 20, but I need 2 more zeros to get to 2000,
so 2 zeros get tagged onto the 5
4 x 4 = 16

Groups	Total
	874
200	- 800
	74
10	- 40
	34
8	- 32
218	2

Let's do the year 874.
2 x 4 = 8, but I need 2 more zeros to get to 800,
so 2 zeros get tagged onto the 2
10 x 4 = 40

8 x 4 = 32 You have to brainstorm what you can
multiply by 4 to get to or close to your number or you can
just take away eight at a time.

We can't take 4 away again and there are 2 left over, so 874 is not a leap year.

Try it with the years 2008 and 1726.

Day 42

Let's say Noah sent out the dove at 10 AM and it stayed out until noon. How long was it gone? Draw each time on the clocks below and then write how much time has elapsed, how much time has gone by.

Elapsed time: Elapsed time: Elapsed time:

Now try with these times. Noon until 4 PM, 4 PM until 10 PM – For these, just draw the new time. You can use the previous clock to help you count the hours.

Let's say the dove flew past after half an hour but stayed out another two hours before it returned. How long did it stay out?

If Noah sent out the dove at 10:00, when did it return? Draw the time.

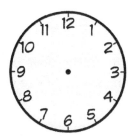

If the dove was sent out at ten in the morning and didn't return until three in the afternoon, how long was it out of the ark?

Draw these times on the clocks and then write how much time passed from the first to the second. 6:30 and 11:00

Elapsed Time:

Let's say Noah sent out the dove at 7:35 and it stayed out until 10:55. How long was the dove out of the ark? Draw the times and then figure out the elapsed time.

       Elapsed time: Elapsed time:

Try again with these times. 11:50 and 12:05, 10:30 and 1:25, 4:15 and 9:40.

       Elapsed time: Elapsed time:

Let's say Noah sent out the dove at 8:02 in the morning and it didn't return until 12:40 in the afternoon. How long was the dove out of the ark?

Try it with these times: 7:46 AM and 11:07 PM, 10:15 PM to 5:47 AM, midnight to noon

Day 43

Use your coins to buy the items. How many ways can you pay for each item?

30¢   18¢   87¢ $0.59 $0.44 $0.91

How many ways can you make one dollar with coins? Write down at least ten different ways.

Add these amounts together. 30¢   18¢   87¢

How much would four trains cost?

Let's say you had five quarters and wanted to buy the train. How much do you have left after you buy the train?

Now try it with these numbers. Buy the Rubrik's Cube with $2.75. Buy the bear with $4.12. Buy sixteen boomerangs with $5.80.

Day 44

Count the worth of each group of coins and bills. One hundred and thirty cents is one dollar and thirty cents. We write it like this. $1.30

Now count your total starting with the highest bill. How much money do you have?

Add the amounts from part A and see if you get the amount in part B.

$1.99
+ $2.99
$4.98

Then double the amount. And again! And again?

Take the amount from part B and multiply it by 2 and by 4 and by 8. Did you get the answers from part C?

Day 45
Review

Divide by four and see if these years are leap years.

Groups	Totals		Groups	Totals
	2018			376

Let's say Noah sent out the dove at 6:12AM and it didn't return until 2:47PM. How long was the dove out of the ark?

You have fifteen dimes, thirteen quarters, forty-three nickels, and twenty-seven pennies. You buy something for $3.75. How much do you have left?

Day 46

If the Tower of Babel were 45 feet tall, and the next tallest building was 23 feet tall, how much taller was the Tower of Babel?

If the Tower of Babel were 57 feet tall, and the next tallest building was 45 feet tall, how much taller was the Tower of Babel?

If the Tower of Babel were twelve feet taller than the previous tallest building which was twenty-five feet tall, then how tall was the Tower of Babel?

If the Tower of Babel were forty-one feet taller than the previous tallest building which was eighteen feet tall, then how tall was the Tower of Babel?

If the Tower of Babel were 425 feet tall, and the next tallest building was 210 feet tall, how much taller was the Tower of Babel?

If the Tower of Babel were 657 feet tall, and the next tallest building was 452 feet tall, how much taller was the Tower of Babel?

If the Tower of Babel were twenty-four meters taller than the previous tallest building which was seventeen meters tall, then how tall was the Tower of Babel?

If the Tower of Babel were forty-nine meters taller than the previous tallest building which was eighteen meters tall, then how tall was the Tower of Babel?

If the Tower of Babel were 52 yards tall, and the next tallest building was 13 yards tall, how much taller was the Tower of Babel?

If the Tower of Babel were 75 yards tall, and the next tallest building was 58 yards tall, how much taller was the Tower of Babel?

If the Tower of Babel were twenty-seven hundred inches (2700 ft) taller than the previous tallest building which was fifteen thousand inches tall, then how tall was the Tower of Babel?

If the Tower of Babel were four times taller than the previous tallest building which was eighty-six feet tall, then how tall was the Tower of Babel?

How many inches are in 17 yards?

How many feet are in 17,700 inches?

Then find out how many yards are in 17,700 inches. Use your answer for feet.

Day 47

If it were 5 miles from Ur to Shechem and 12 miles from
Shechem to the Negev, how far did Abraham travel all together?

If it were 52 kilometers from Ur to Shechem and 27 miles from
Shechem to the Negev, how far did Abraham travel all together?

If the trip was 18 miles and the first part was 7 miles,
how long was the second part of the trip?

If the trip was 78 kilometers and the first part was
43 kilometers, how long was the second part of the trip?

If it were 55 miles from Ur to Shechem and 19 miles from
Shechem to the Negev, how far did Abraham travel all together?

If it were 247 kilometers from Ur to Shechem and 37 miles from
Shechem to the Negev, how far did Abraham travel all together?

If the trip was 180 miles and the first part was 90 miles,
how long was the second part of the trip?

If the trip was 385 kilometers and the first part was
143 kilometers, how long was the second part of the trip?

If it were 512 miles from Ur to Shechem and 128 miles from
Shechem to the Negev, how far did Abraham travel all together?

If it were 328 kilometers from Ur to Shechem and 380 miles
from Shechem to the Negev, how far did Abraham travel all together?

If the trip was 180 miles and the first part was 77 miles,
how long was the second part of the trip?

If the trip was 758 kilometers and the first part was
429 kilometers, how long was the second part of the trip?

If it were 2755 miles from Ur to Shechem and 1239 miles from
Shechem to the Negev, how far did Abraham travel all together?

If it were 2975 kilometers from Ur to Shechem and 3762 miles from
Shechem to the Negev, how far did Abraham travel all together?

If the trip was 384 miles and the first part was 145 miles,
how long was the second part of the trip?

If the trip was 824 kilometers and the first part was
346 kilometers, how long was the second part of the trip?

Day 48

Abraham is on a journey. Draw a line that is one inch long. Draw a line that is three centimeters long. Which is longer?

Now draw Abraham's journey. Use the ruler. How long did you draw your line?

Draw a line that's three and a half inches long. Then draw one that is six and a half centimeters long. Which is longer?

Now draw Abraham's journey. How long did you draw your line?

Draw five lines or measure five small things in your house and write down their measurement in centimeters. There are ten lines for each centimeter. We can write tenths like this.

0.1 one tenth, 0.2 two tenths, 0.3 three tenths, etc. Each line is one tenth. Just count them up. If it measured seven centimeters and then eight more little lines, the answer would be 7.8.

Now measure those five things with inches and write down their measurements. You'll use fractions this time. There are sixteen lines for each inch.

8 lines would be $8/16$ or ½   4 lines would be $4/16$ or ¼

2 lines would be $2/16$ or $1/8$ 3 lines would be $3/16$

If it measured 5 inches and 5 little lines, the answer would be 5 $5/16$. That's called a mixed number when the number is part whole number and part fraction.

Day 49

10   11   12   13   14   15   16   17   18   19   20

Round to the nearest ten.

31 →   58 →   42 →   17 →

When a number ends in a 5, it's right in the middle of the number line. We just make the decision to always round it up. So 25 rounds up to 30, 35 rounds up to 40, 45 rounds up to 50, etc.

13 →   35 →   46 →   65 →

100   110   120   130   140   150   160   170   180   190   200

Round the numbers below to the nearest hundred.

143 →   450 →   129 →   680 →

Round these numbers to the closest hundred.

264 →   949 →   150 →   618 →

Day 50
Review

There are three feet in every yard. How many feet are in 47 yards.

There are 12 inches in every foot. How many inches are in 23 yards?

How many feet are in 13,452 inches?

If it were 2463 miles from Ur to Shechem and 2394 miles from Shechem to the Negev, how far did Abraham travel all together?

If the trip was 742 kilometers and the first part was 460 kilometers, how long was the second part of the trip?

Measure three things with inches and write down their measurements with fractions. If it measured 5 inches and 5 little lines, the answer would be $5 \frac{5}{16}$.

Round these numbers to the closest hundred.

349 ➔   838 ➔   250 ➔   609 ➔

Day 51

- 144   can of Coke
- 108   homemade biscuit
- 68   slice of bread
- 240   package of M&Ms
- 110   Cheerios (1 ¼ cups)
- 51   homemade chocolate chip cookies
- 140   goldfish, 45 crackers
- 377   one cup of soft vanilla ice cream
- 188   one slice of cheese pizza, Dominos
- 111   one scrambled egg with butter and milk
- 80   apple
- 71   orange
- 117   one cup of apple juice
- 406   extra-crispy chicken thigh from KFC
- 520   quarter-pounder with cheese from McDonald's
- 288   4 ounces of lean ground beef
- 190   a serving of salted peanuts

Let's say that you ate a homemade biscuit, an apple, and a scrambled egg. How many calories did you consume?

How many calories did you eat if you had an orange and Cheerios for breakfast?

If you had two chocolate chip cookies, how many calories did you eat?

How many calories did you consume if you at a quarter-pounder with cheese from McDonald's and an extra-cripsy chicken thigh from KFC and a chocolate chip cookie?

Plan out breakfast, lunch, and dinner. Choose at least three foods "to eat" for each meal. Then figure out the calorie total of each meal.

Total your calories for the day.

If you ate that every day for seven days, how many calories would you have consumed?

Now figure it out for 4 and 9 days.

Add up all the calories in the list!

If you ate all that each day for thirteen days, how many calories would that be?

Double it by adding and find the number of calories for twenty-six days.

If you had 57 slices of bread over the month, how many calories from bread did you consume?

Day 52

If a man was sixty-eight years old, how long ago was he three years old?

How old he was fifty-seven years from the time he was three.

If the man was forty-nine years old, how long ago was he three?

If an animal was 47 months old, how old would she be in 8 months?

Let's say we're trying to get to 50. We have 31. Subtract 31 from 50 to see how much more we need.

Try it with these numbers: 50 – 12, 50 – 24, 20 - 8

If twenty-seven animals were all eight years old, how many years total had they all been alive?

What if there had been seventy-six of them?

If a man was one hundred three years old, how old was he eighteen years ago?

If the man was one hundred ten years old, how old was he thirty-eight years ago?

What is the average number of years these cows lived? Find the number of years for each by finding the difference between the year they were born and the year they died. Add the ages together. Divide by the total number of animals. That's how you'll find the average. (There were some old cows. The average would be more like 18-22 years.)

Born: 1904   Died: 1927
Born: 1894   Died: 1924
Born: 1889   Died: 1911
Born: 1884   Died: 1917

Day 53

If Abraham had lived in Canaan from January 3rd to January 27th, how long had he lived there?

If Abraham lived in Canaan from January 3rd until the end of the month, how long did he live there?

Now how many days did he live there, if he lived there all of January and until February 15th?

How many days did he live there if he was in Canaan during all of March, April, May, and June?

How many days did Abraham live in Canaan if he lived there just during the months of January, March, June, and December?

If Abraham lived in Canaan from January first through the end of March, how many days did he stay? (no leap year)

If he ended up staying 21 days less than that, how long did he live there?

If Abraham lived there for thirty-four weeks, how many days did he stay?

If Abraham lived there for forty-six weeks, how many days did he stay?

If Abraham lived there for forty-three days less than one hundred days, how many days did he stay?

If Abraham lived there for thirty-two days less than one hundred fourteen days, how many days did he stay?

If Abraham only stayed there for two weeks, how many hours is that?

If Abraham lived there for the months of July and August, how many hours is that?

If Abraham lived there for three years, how many days was that? (no leap year)

If he only stayed one hundred fifty-seven days less than that, how long did he stay?

Day 54

Multiply.

10 x 5 =   20 x 5 =   15 x 10 =   25 x 8 =

124 x 3 =   426 x 9 =

278 x 7 =   379 x 6 =

14 x 35 =   46 x 29 =

28 x 71 =   39 x 67 =

Day 55

Review   Calories

406   extra-crispy chicken thigh
188   one slice of cheese pizza
111   one scrambled egg with butter and milk

Add up all the calories in the list above and find out how many calories you would have consumed if you ate that every day for twenty-four days.

Find the average of the group of numbers.

556, 588, 560, 532, 569

If Abraham stayed there for three weeks, how many hours is that?

If Abraham lived there for the months of June and July, how many hours is that?

If he stayed 275 hours less than that, how long did he stay?

Multiply.   45 x 23 =   76 x 19 =

Day 56

If Sarah were 93 and Abraham 99, <u>about</u> how old is that added together?

Try it with these numbers. Estimate the answers.

$42 + 48 =$ $51 + 59 =$ $27 + 31 =$ $94 + 91 =$

Estimate. About how much is 78 + 63?

Now try with these numbers: 44 + 75, 15 + 57, 39 + 26

Estimate. About how much is 159 - 76? (Pay attention.)

Now try with these numbers: 170 - 29, 114 - 68, 155 - 82.

Estimate the time passed. If 120 minutes passed, then 254 minutes, and then another 531 minutes. About how many hours is that?

Now estimate the number of hours with these numbers by rounding to the nearest hundred: 204 minutes and 423 minutes, and 720 minutes and 756 minutes.

Day 57

Draw 6:30, three thirty, and half past ten.

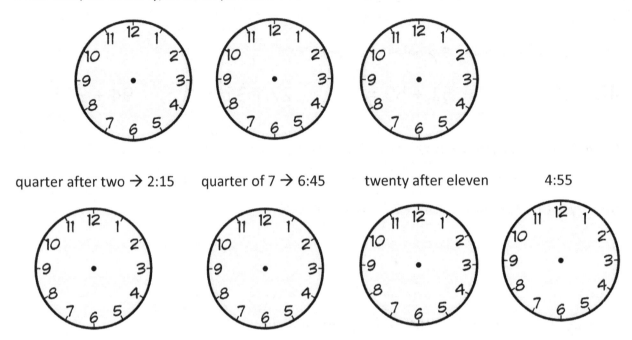

quarter after two → 2:15   quarter of 7 → 6:45   twenty after eleven   4:55

Draw 7:17 on the second clock below. How much time elapses from 3:34 to 7:42 if both times are PM on the same day?

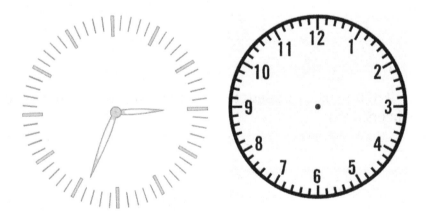

If 7:42 were in the AM the next morning, how much time would have passed from 3:34 the previous afternoon?

How much time elapses between 3:34 PM and 7:17 PM the same day?

How much time elapses between 2:12 AM and 5:03 PM on the same day?

Day 58

hundreds	tens	ones
1	0	0
+	9	0
1	9	0

Add together. Make sure to add together the correct place values.

$200 + 500 =$ $40 + 50 =$ $210 + 6 =$ $105 + 3 =$

tens	ones
10	0
9	0

hundreds	tens	ones
1	0	0
	10	0
		100

Subtract:

$140 - 70 =$ $120 - 80 =$ $150 - 90 =$ $110 - 30 =$

Subtract 142 – 85. Here are two ways to look at it. What did I do in each example?

```
 142
-  85
  60
 -  3
  57
```

hundreds	tens	ones
	13	12
	- 8	5
	5	7

Subtract and find the difference.

$240 - 152 =$ $424 - 185 =$

326 – 97 =   126 – 89 =

Add twenty thousand four hundred and seventy-four thousand nine hundred.

Add 5,236 + 1,985.   Add 4,914 + 7,286.

Find the difference.   1,235 – 859   5,246 – 2,577

Day 59

Let's do righteous/unrighteous fractions. Draw a square and draw a line to divide it in half. Color in one half. We write fractions like this:

$\frac{1}{2}$ or when typing I write them like this ½ or like this $^1/_2$

Draw a line through the middle of those rectangles from side to side. Color in one more box. How many of the four boxes are colored in?

If there were two people and one was righteous, how could you write as a fraction how many of the people were righteous?

How would you write the fraction that would show how many were unrighteous?

Write the fraction that would show the number of unrighteous people if there were four people all together and only one was unrighteous.

Write the fraction that would show the number of righteous if there were three people and only one was righteous.

Write the fraction that would show the number of unrighteous in that scenario.

Let's say that there was a group of eight people. Let's say that five were righteous. Write the number of righteous and the number of unrighteous as fractions. Then use the > greater than sign or the < less than sign to show which fraction is greater (which animal has more

Do it again with a group of 13 all together and 7 are unrighteous.

Draw a horizontal line across the middle of the rectangle. Then draw a vertical line down the middle of the rectangle. Divide each side in half with another vertical line. Divide each of those boxes in half with another vertical line in each one. You should have sixteen boxes, eight on top and eight on bottom. Lightly color in half of the big rectangle. Make sure you can still see all the lines. Write down as many fractions as you can that could be represented by that half. For instance, one half is colored in, but so are two out of the four bigger inside boxes, what else? Those are called equivalent fractions. They are all equal amounts, just written different ways.

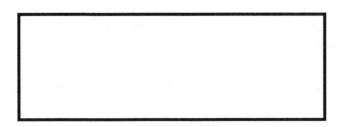

2/4 + 2/4 =   4/8 + 4/8 =   8/16 + 8/16 =

Day 60
Review

Estimate: 276 ÷ 4 Estimate the answer by rounding to the nearest hundred, then rounding to the nearest ten, and then find the exact answer.

How much time elapses between 4:17 AM and 1:53 PM on the same day?

Add thirty thousand five hundred and sixty-eight thousand seven hundred.

Add 2,193 + 3,847   Find the difference 5,246 – 2,577

List six fractions that are equivalent to one half. two fourths...seven fourteenths

18/36 + 18/36 =

12/24 + 12/24 =

Day 61

_____ x 8 = 296   7 x _____ = 378

_____ ÷ 5 = 718   _____ ÷ 7 = 254

_____ x 8 = 136   6 x _____ = 252

_____ ÷ 8 = 329   _____ ÷ 4 = 183

Day 62

1586	$10.00	5185	$10.00
+ 785	- $5.30	+ 3078	- $4.87

Divide by four and see if these years are leap years.

Groups	Totals		Groups	Totals
	1876			1324

Let's say Noah sent out the dove at 7:32AM and it didn't return until 2:45PM. How long was the dove out of the ark?

You have thirteen dimes, fifteen quarters, fifty-two nickels, and twenty-six pennies. You buy something for $3.75. How much do you have left?

Day 63

526	$10.00	8276	$10.00
+ 798	- $3.90	+ 1957	- $1.36

What's $5/7$ (84)?

245	587
x 61	x 43

Day 64

2417	$10.00	5395	$10.00
+ 690	- $2.70	+ 4878	- $3.16

There are three feet in every yard. How many feet are in 72 yards.

There are 12 inches in every foot. How many inches are in 18 yards? (Hint: First figure out how many feet.)

Twenty-four inches is two feet. 24 ÷ 12 = 2

How many feet are in 5,892 inches?

Day 65

2367	$10.00	395	$10.00
+ 698	- $3.60	x 78	- $4.72

What's $^4/_9$ (243)?

Use a Groups and Totals chart to divide 425 by five.

Day 66 (ruler)

If it were 4162 miles from Ur to Shechem and 3598 miles from Shechem to the Negev, how far did Abraham travel all together?

If the trip was 862 kilometers and the first part was 630 kilometers, how long was the second part of the trip?

Round these numbers to the closest hundred.

350 →   757 →   325 →   649 →

$2/9 + 3/9 =$ $3/11 + 7/11 =$

$4/9 + 5/9 =$ $3/12 + 3/12 =$

List three fractions equivalent to $6/12$.

Draw a line that's $3 \, 5/16$ inches long.

Day 67

What's $\frac{9}{14}(364)$?   How many groups of 23 are in 1104?

Calories
51   homemade chocolate chip cookies

Add up all the calories consumed if all 15 members of a soccer team each ate three chocolate chip cookies.

Find the average of the group of numbers.

556, 588, 560, 532

If Abraham stayed there for three weeks, how many hours is that?

Day 68

What's $\frac{5}{12}$ (780)?   How many groups of 16 are in 560?

Estimate: 284 ÷ 4 Estimate the answer by rounding to the nearest hundred. Then estimate the answer by rounding to the nearest ten. Then find the exact answer.

Add thirty thousand four hundred and seventy-nine thousand six.

Add 4,132 + 3,957   Find the difference 6,415 − 3,772

Day 69

Let's say Abraham's visitors were with him from 5:50 in the morning until 3:17 in the afternoon. How long were they with Abraham? Draw the times and find the elapsed time.

   Elapsed time:

If Abraham lived there from June through August, how many hours is that?

If he stayed 275 hours less than that, how long did he stay?

Multiply.

45 x 36 =   76 x 22 =

Day 70

8497	$10.00	826	$10.00
+ 543	- $4.16	x 18	- $5.72

What's $^9/_4$ (144)?

Use a Groups and Totals chart to divide 322 by seven.

Day 71

Write the fraction one half, one third, two thirds, and three fourths, and draw pictures to show the fractions.

How much is one third plus one third?

Write the equation and answer and draw a picture to show it.

Now add one quarter and three quarters and draw pictures. What's the answer?

If God destroyed one third of five different cities, how much did God destroy? 5(1/3) How do you solve that?

Try it with one third of seven cities.

What if He destroyed half of one third of the cities?

Now try with three quarters of a third of the cities.

Divide the numerator and denominator by three to find an equivalent fraction.

Day 72

Draw a picture and write a fraction that shows each of the following fractions: one half, one third, one fourth, one fifth, one sixth.

Can you draw a picture to show one and one half? How do you think you write one and one half?

Write three and two thirds, four and five sixths, and twelve and three sevenths.

Find the sum or difference.   Examples: $3\frac{1}{2} + 2\frac{1}{2} = 5\,\frac{2}{2}$ = 5 and 1 = 6

$1\frac{1}{4} - \frac{3}{4} = (\frac{4}{4} \text{ and } \frac{1}{4}) - \frac{3}{4} = \frac{5}{4} - \frac{3}{4} = \frac{2}{4} = \frac{1}{2}$

$\frac{2}{6} + \frac{4}{6} =$ $\frac{1}{5} + \frac{2}{5} =$

$\frac{2}{3} - \frac{1}{3} =$ $\frac{4}{6} - \frac{3}{6} =$

$23\,\frac{2}{6} + 24\,\frac{3}{6} =$ $18\,\frac{3}{7} + 5\,\frac{1}{7} =$

$4\,\frac{4}{6} - 1\,\frac{3}{6} =$ $14\,\frac{5}{6} - 7\,\frac{1}{6} =$

$3/5 + 2/5 =$

$2/3 + 2/3 =$
Draw a picture to show why.

$1\ 3/7 + 5\ 4/7 =$

$4\ 1/6 + 6\ 5/6 =$

$1\ 1/6 - 5/6 =$

$10\ 1/5 - 5\ 4/5 =$

Day 73

Draw ten circles. Color in one of them. How do you think you would write the fraction to show that number?

Color in one more and write a fraction to show that number. Then keep doing it until all the circles are colored in.

A tenth can be written as a decimal as well. It looks like this.   0.1

How do you think you would write two tenths?

Write each tenth fraction as a decimal.

0.1 is the same as 0.10. That's the same as $0.10. That's the same as ten cents. How much is ten dimes?

Write addition and subtraction equations as either fractions or decimals. Answer all of them. Here are examples. To add decimals. We add just like regular numbers but make sure the decimal point stays in the same place.

$.2 + .5 =$

$4/10 + 5/10 =$

$.1 + .5 =$

$2/10 + 6/10 =$

$.4 - .3 =$

$8/10 - 7/10 =$

Add together each decimal and each fraction from one tenth to ten tenths all together. What are the answers?

Remember .5 Add normally, but keep the decimal place in the same spot.
$$\begin{array}{r} .5 \\ +\ .5 \\ \hline 1.0 \end{array}$$

$$\begin{array}{r} 1.7 \\ +\quad 2.5 \\ \hline 4.2 \end{array}$$ The decimal point goes straight down into the answer. This is just about keeping your place values together. You add tenths to tenths. That's the name of the place value to the right of the decimal point, tenths.

As fractions these are...

$^5/_{10} + {}^5/_{10} = {}^{10}/_{10} = 1$

Add these decimals. Solve. Then write the equations as a fraction and show how you would solve it.

.4 + .8 =

2.8 + 3.2 =

5.3 + 4.7 =

2.6 + 9.6 =

Day 74

You can write one tenth as a decimal as well.   0.1

How would you write two tenths?

0.1 is the same as 0.10. That's the same as $0.10. That's the same as ten cents. How do you think you would write twenty cents?

Write thirty, forty, fifty, sixty, seventy, eighty, ninety, and one hundred cents.

Now let's add those together. Start with ten cents plus twenty cents. $0.10
                                                                          + $0.20

Keep going. Add on thirty cents then forty cents...

Multiply those answers by 7.

Start with $150.00 and then spend those amounts. Do you have enough money?

Day 75
Review

Solve and simplify into mixed numbers. Don't leave an improper fraction in the answer.

$4(^3/_5) =$

$7 \, ^1/_4 - 4 \, ^5/_8 =$

$8 \, ^1/_3 - 3 \, ^4/_6 =$

$5 \, (^6/_7) =$

$5 \, ^2/_6 - 1 \, ^3/_6 =$

$^1/_5 + \, ^6/_{10} =$

$6.7 + 1.6 =$

$\begin{array}{r} \$12.00 \\ - \, \$2.30 \\ \hline \end{array}$

Day 76

Find the difference using these numbers.

150 – 80 =   160 – 90 =   130 – 60 =   120 – 40 =

If you had 123 books at home and took fifty to the library, how many books did you still have at home?

If you had 123 books at home and took 55 to the library, how many books did you still have at home?

Find the difference using these numbers.

123 – 64, 145 – 58, 127 – 39, 114 – 37

If you bought books at the library book sale for $2.57, and paid for it with $5.00. How much change did you get? Below is also an example using $50 and $25.75.

4.9 1	49 1	499 1	49.9 1
$5.00	500	5000	$50.00
- $2.57	-257	-2575	-$25.75
	243	2425	$24.25

Find the difference. 600 – 45, 7000 – 2345, $20.00 - $15.75, $10.00 - $3.62

Day 77

This is how you write ten cents. 10 ¢ or $0.10

This is how you write five cents and one cent. 5 ¢ or $0.05   1 ¢ or $0.01

What are these coins? What are their names and how much are they worth? Write the amount they are worth using a dollar sign.

Count up the value of these coins. Write the amount with a dollar sign.

_____

_____

Write down five cents plus five cents equals ten cents in a different way.
      5 ¢ + 5 ¢ = 10 ¢

Combine coins that equal a dollar into two piles. Write down at least two equations. Use a dollar sign. Example: $0.50 + $0.50 = $1.00

Then write two subtraction equations using what you just wrote.
Example: $1.00 - $0.50 = $0.50

To subtract from one dollar, you need to be able to subtract from 100. Do you see the similarity?
100 and $1.00

$2.13
+ $1.49
$.

What's 100 – 40? Look at the example below. It's just like subtracting 10 – 4. Can you see it?

```
100          100
- 40         - 43
 60           60
             - 3
              57
```

What's $1.00 - $0.40?   What's $1.00 - $0.43?

Subtract. Then check to see if your answers make sense! Add the answer and what you subtracted together, even use coins to do it. Do they make a dollar?

$1.00 $1.00 $1.00 $1.00 $1.00
-$0.30   -$0.53   -$0.78   -$0.16   -$0.24

$0.90 $5.00 $1.18 $10.00 $6.50
+$0.30   -$1.29   +$0.88   - $0.46   +$3.74

Day 78

If Isaac was born at 6 AM and eight days later was circumcised at noon, how old was he to the hour, eight days and how many hours?

How many hours are there from 8 AM until 4 PM?

Draw two times and write how much time passes between them.

Elapsed time:

If he had been born at 12:30 AM and was circumcised at noon eight days later, how old was he to the minute?

How many minutes pass from 12:15 PM until 1:00 PM? How long is it from 5:15 AM until 3:30 PM?

How long is it from 8:45 AM until 1:30 PM? Draw two times and write how much time passes between them.

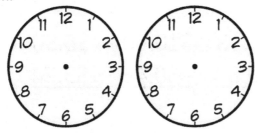

Elapsed time:

Eight days passed. How many hours is that?   How many minutes is that?

If it had been eighteen days, how many hours would that have been?

If one hundred and eighteen days had passed, how many hours would that have been? To figure that out we just multiply the parts and add them back together.

Try it with these numbers.   315 x 24 and 264 x 17

If you need the practice, try another. 214 x 35

Day 79

If Ishmael and Isaac each got one half of ten dollars, how much would they each get?

one hundred dollars: $1000:   one dollar:

50 cents: 50 dollars: 500 dollars:

Find half of these numbers by multiplying by .5, which to do that you just multiply by 5 and then add a decimal place to your answer.   63, 153, 4931, 784

You are going to divide up the inheritance another way. Divide these numbers to find the answers. Let's say Ishmael gets the remainder, whatever is left over. For instance, 9 divided by 2 gives us 4 with one left over. That's the remainder. We can write the answer as 4 r 1.

$23 \div 4 =$ $238 \div 4 =$ $2388 \div 4 =$

$56 \div 7 =$ $562 \div 7 =$ $5629 \div 7 =$

Day 80
Review

Find the difference.   800 – 53   9000 – 1827

Add and subtract. Then check to see if your answers make sense.

$8.00	$1.84	$10.00	$7.50
-$3.17	+$0.78	- $0.32	+$3.50

Multiply.   538 x 46

Divide.

614 ÷ 9 =   215 ÷ 4 =   6290 ÷ 8 =

Day 81

Let's look at the lay of the land. Let's look at shapes. I'm going to show you shapes, and you tell me what they are and how you know.

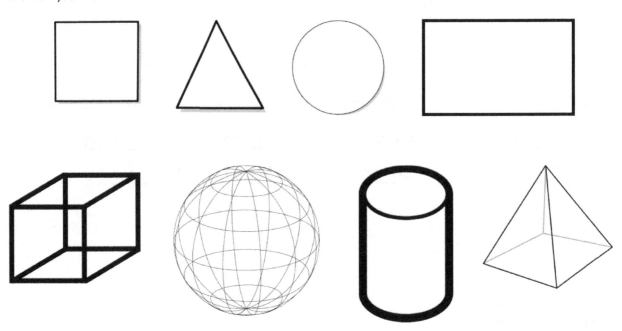

A polygon is a flat, closed figure with straight sides.

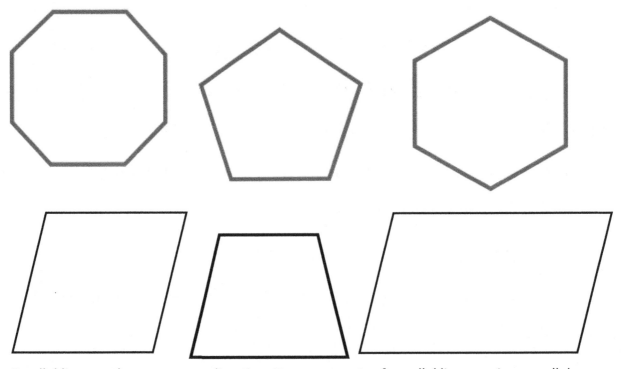

<u>Parallel lines</u> go the same exact direction. How many sets of parallel lines are in a parallelogram (shown on the right)?

Day 82

```
   56              12             74
 - 14            + 35           - 43
 ────            ────           ────
```

```
   50             217            272            79
 - 34           + 75          - 156          + 47
 ────           ─────         ──────         ────
```

Do the opposite to check my work.

$225 \div 15 = 15$ $2788 \div 34 = 81$ $735 \div 5 = 149$ $2104 \div 8 = 263$

Answer the question and the do the opposite to check the work.

$305 \div 5 =$ $384 \div 16 =$ $1029 \div 3 =$

Day 83

We're going to convert fractions into decimals. Follow the pattern to convert the fractions into decimals.

$^1/_{10}$ $^2/_{10}$ $^3/_{10}$ $^4/_{10}$ $^5/_{10}$ $^6/_{10}$ $^7/_{10}$ $^8/_{10}$ $^9/_{10}$

0.1   0.2   0.3   0.4

Do the opposite. Convert the decimals into fractions.

0.1   0.2   0.3   0.4   0.5   0.6   0.7   0.8   0.9

Write these numbers as decimals and then convert them to mixed numbers: seven and one tenth, eight and seven tenths, twelve and nine tenths, five and five tenths.

Compare the first two and the last two numbers (that you just wrote). Draw a greater than and less than symbol between them.

What else does five out of ten equal? How else could you write five tenths and have it mean the same amount?

Write as decimals 57 hundredths, 4 and 17 hundredths, 28 and 3 hundredths, 189 and 9 tenths. Compare the first two numbers and the last two numbers.

Now convert them to fractions or mixed numbers.

Day 84

The first rectangle is all the wood together in its bundle. That represents how big it is. Divide the next rectangle in half. Color in one half of it. Divide the next rectangle by four. Color in one quarter. Divide the last rectangle by three. Draw two lines to make three parts. Color in one third.

Use the greater than/less than symbol to show which is biggest in each pair.

We write one half like this. $^1/_2$ We write two halves like this. $^2/_2$ $^2/_2 = 1$ $^{100}/_{100} = 1$

How many quarters do you need to make a half? How do you write 2 out of 4 parts as a fraction?

How many quarters do you need to make a whole?

How do you write 4 out of 4 parts as a fraction? What whole number does $^4/_4$ equal?

What's bigger: three fourths or one? Write your answer using < or >.

Write an addition and a subtraction equation that give the answer $^3/_4$.

Now write an addition equation and a subtraction equation with the answer $^3/_8$.

½ x 10   or   ½ (10)   or   ½ * 10   These are a half of ten. Write an equation that would give you a quarter of sixteen.

To solve $1/4$ (16) you would multiply sixteen times one and then divide by four. Or, you could divide sixteen by four and then multiply by one. It doesn't matter which order you do it in. What's the answer?

How would you solve $3/4$ (16)? What's the answer?

What's $2/5$ (35)?

$3/5$ (225) =

$4/9$ (315) =

$2/7$ (161) =

Day 85
Review

Identify how many sets of parallel lines are in the shapes.

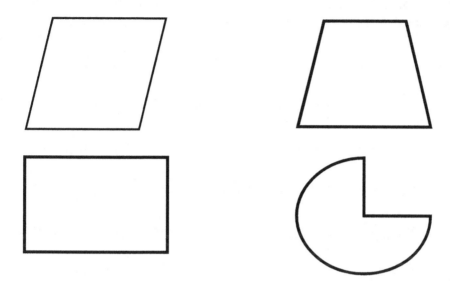

Add and subtract. Then do the opposite to see if your answers make sense.

$5.00 $1.32 $10.00
-$1.24   +$0.78   - $3.72

Answer the question and the do the opposite to check the work.

810 ÷ 18 =

Write the value of a penny, a nickel, a dime, and a quarter as decimals.

Write as decimals 67 hundredths, 1 and 1 hundredth, 280 and 9 hundredths, 289 and 3 tenths. Compare the first two numbers and the last two numbers.

Now convert them to fractions.

How much change from a ten dollar bill would you receive if you bought something for $6.28?

What's $^4/_7$ (35)?

Subtract one quarter from one. Write the equation and answer.

Day 86

A bag of potatoes weighing a kilogram has about seven potatoes inside. A slice of bread is about 29 grams. Which estimate is best for these items?

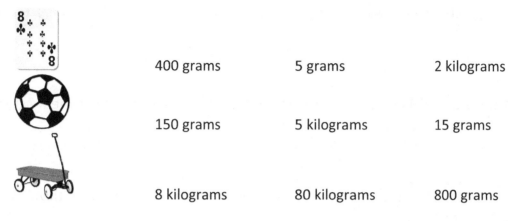

400 grams	5 grams	2 kilograms
150 grams	5 kilograms	15 grams
8 kilograms	80 kilograms	800 grams

A gram is one thousandth of a kilogram. A kilogram is one thousand grams. Write these measures as the other.

2000 grams   4 kilograms

500 grams   1.5 kilograms

A pound is sixteen ounces. An ounce is one sixteenth of a pound. Write the measures as the other.

128 ounces   27 pounds

320 ounces   139 pounds

Day 87

If all together the ram and altar weighed 14 kilograms and the ram weighed 5 kilograms, how much did the altar weigh without the ram?

If the altar weighed 153 tons and 25 tons of ram was on top, how much did it all weigh together?

If all together it weighed 351 grams, how much did the ram weigh if the altar alone weighed 327 grams?

If the altar weighed 209 ounces and the ram weighed 57 ounces, how much did the altar weigh after the ram was placed on it?

If the altar weighed eight times as much as the ram on it and the ram was 73 tons, how much did the altar weigh?

If the altar weighed five times as much as the ram at 67 ounces, how much did it weigh?

If the altar weighed forty-seven times the weight of the ram on it, how much did it weigh if the ram is fifteen ounces.

If the altar weighs 64 times the weight of the ram on it, and the ram is 320 grams, how much does the altar weigh?

If the ram weighed half of what the altar weighed, how much did it weigh if the altar weighed 1528 grams?

If the ram on the altar weighed one sixth of the altar, then how much did it weigh if the altar weighed 468 tons?

If the ram weighed one twelfth of the altar, how much did it weigh if the altar weighed 2592 grams?

If the ram weighed one fifteenth of the altar, how much did they weigh if the altar was 675 pounds?

Day 88

Draw a line on the page. Then use a ruler to measure it to the nearest inch.

Then draw lines that are three inches long, five inches long, and seven inches long.

Add together your measurements.

Draw lines that are two centimeters, four centimeters, and eight centimeters long. Are those numbers all odd or even?

Add together those measurements.

Now measure the line you drew to the nearest tenth of a centimeter. If it measures four lines past the number six on the ruler, then it would measure 7.4 centimeters.

Now draw lines that are 1.8 cm, 3.2 cm, 5.5 cm.

Add together those measurements.

Day 89

If we bought the toy for five dollars and sold the toy for eight dollars, how much profit did we make? This is how you write that with a dollar sign. **$3.00**

Figure out your profit. Buy at $4.00 and sell at $8.00.

Buy at twelve dollars and sell at twenty-six dollars.

Buy at twenty-one cents and sell at forty-five cents.

Buy at $0.35 and sell at $0.79.

Buy at $6.35, and sell at $10.50.

Buy at $24.23, and sell at $37.45.

Buy at $112.03, and sell at $150.22.

Buy at $46.18, and sell at $61.25.

What happens when you have negative cents after you subtract? Look at this example. Buy at $1.20, and sell at $3.15. These are all the same.

$3.15	315	315	315	315
- $1.20	- 120	-120	-120	-120
2.00	200	205	200	205
-.10	-10	- 10	190	195
+.05	5	195	195	
$1.95	195			

Find your profit. Buy at $15.02, and sell at $23.15. Buy at $13.67, and sell at $46.19.

Buy at $53.69, and sell at $80.50. Buy at $23.85, and sell at $30.80.

Find your profit. Buy at $234.20, and sell at $523.00. Buy at $416.36, and sell at $500.00.

Buy at $397.62, and sell at $615.50. Buy at $481.68, and sell at $700.00.

Day 90
Review

Find your profit. Buy at $379.40, and sell at $523.00. Buy at $382.46, and sell at $500.00.

If the ram weighed one twelfth of the altar, how much did it weigh if the altar weighed 2016 pounds?

If the ram weighed one sixteenth of the altar, how much did it weigh if the altar was 944 kilograms?

Draw a line that is 2.3 cm.

A pound is sixteen ounces. An ounce is one sixteenth of a pound. Write the measures as the other.

176 ounces   34 pounds

Day 91

We don't know how many people were there to witness the transaction. If there were 9 people there and 7 came, how many would have been there? If there were fifteen and seven left, how many would be there? If there were 80 and 40 more came, how many would be in attendance? If there were 130 and 60 left, how many would remain? Let's say there are 140. What if 80 left? How many would still be there? Now, figure out how many would still be there if these left: 10, 4, 7, and 13.

If there were 100 people and 3 left, how many would be remaining?

How many people would still be there if 30 left, or 37, or 74?

What if there were 248 people there and five times more came. How many people would be there?

Let's say that there were 1000 people and 8 left. How many people remained there?

How many people would remain if 80 left, or 83, or 860, or 271?

Now let's say there are 1152 people and they were divided into 16 groups. If one of those groups left, how many people would still be there?

Day 92

$23/100 = 23\%$ % is the percent sign

$37/100 =$ $14/100 =$ $6/100 =$ $75/100 =$

How many cents are in one dollar?   What percent of a dollar is one penny?

What percent of a dollar is one nickel?   What percent of a dollar is one dime?

What percent of a dollar is one quarter?

Write the fraction, the percent, and the money amount in dollars for each of the coin amounts above. Do it for one dollar as well.

What's 10% of one dollar? What's 10% of ten dollars? What's 10% of one hundred dollars?

What's an equivalent fraction of $10/100$ with a denominator of 10?

What's ten percent of $2.40?

What percent of one dollar is $5.00?

Day 93

Write down ten. Can you draw a decimal point to turn it into a 1?

Now figure out how much money you would earn from your investment of twenty dollars, fifty dollars, and eighty dollars.

Write $10.00 x 10 = $100.00 and watch what happens to the decimal point.

A percent is a part of a whole, like a fraction.   What's ten percent of $100? $10
                                                          What's ten percent of $10? $1
                                                          What's ten percent of $1 $0.10
                                                          What's ten percent of $0.10 $0.01

Figure out how much money you would have after your investment.

7 dollars at 10% =   7 dollars at 1% =

200 dollars at 10% =   200 dollars at 1% =

Now find the difference between what you earned at ten and one percent.

To find 20% we just find the answer to ten percent and then multiply by two. To find 5% we just find one percent by moving the decimal point and then multiply by five.

Find 1, 5, 10, 15, 20, and 25 percent of $10.00.

$10.00 →

How would you find 34% of $10?

Day 94

34,526 x 5 =   34,526 x 10 =

34,526 x 50 =   34,526 x 100 =

34,526 x 500 =   34,526 x 1000 =

34,526 x 5000 =

34,526 x 5555 =

How would you figure out what's 34,526 x 6666? (Think! Don't multiply.)

$36 \left(\frac{1}{2}\right) =$ $36 \left(\frac{2}{3}\right) =$

$126 \left(\frac{5}{14}\right) =$ $216 \left(\frac{4}{9}\right) =$

Day 95
Review

Let's say that there were 1000 people and 4 were removed. How many people remained?

How many people would remain if 347 of those 1000 left?

Now let's say there are 598 people and they are divided into 13 groups. If one of those groups were removed, how many people would remain?

What's ten percent of $7.20?   What percent of one dollar is $8.00?

$4/4 \times 2/9 =$ $3/7 \times 4/5 =$

$192(3/24) =$ $322 (4/7) =$

Day 96

Solve and simplify into mixed numbers. Don't leave an improper fraction in the answer.

$4(^3/_5) =$

$5\,^1/_3 - 2\,^1/_6 =$

$6\,^1/_3 - 1\,^7/_{12} =$

$451 \times 38 =$

Day 97
Review

$7.00	$4.74	$10.00	$6.50
-$2.63	+$0.89	- $0.26	+$3.75

Write as decimals 48 hundredths, 471 and 6 hundredths.

Now convert them to fractions.

392 x 64 =

Day 98
Review

Write these numbers and then read them out loud.
millions , hundred thousand | ten thousand | thousand , hundreds | tens | ones

four hundred twenty-nine thousand, four hundred three

twelve million six hundred seventy-four thousand thirteen

Solve and simplify into mixed numbers. Don't leave an improper fraction in the answer.

$3/8 \times 5/7 =$

$3 \, 2/6 - 1 \, 1/4 =$

$1/4 + 7/8 =$

$7.7 + 4.9 =$

Multiply.

$394 \times 76 =$

Day 99
Review

$$5013$$
$$- \ 2738$$

$$\$21.78$$
$$- \ \$17.90$$

Write ten thirds and ten ninths each as a mixed number and an improper fraction. Add the improper fractions and add the mixed numbers. Convert the improper fraction into a mixed number. Do the answers match?

257 x 43 =

Day 100
Review

Find the sum or difference. Then do the opposite to see if your answers make sense.

$5.00
-$2.74

$9.65
+$0.78

$10.00
- $4.61

Let's say you had four hundred fifty-six dollars of debt and got one thousand dollars. How much money would you have after you paid your debt?

3500 ÷ 20 =

Day 101
Review

Draw three shapes, ones that have 2, 1, and 0 sets of parallel lines.

478 x 36 =

Answer the question and the do the opposite to check the work.

468 ÷ 18 =

Day 102
Review

Find your profit. Buy at $273.96, and sell at $500.00.

If the ram on the altar weighed one twelfth of the altar, how much did it weigh if the altar weighed 4164 ounces?

Draw a line that is 2.3 cm.

Day 103
Review

If the ram weighed one sixteenth of the altar, how much did it weigh if the altar was 448 pounds?

A pound is sixteen ounces. An ounce is one sixteenth of a pound. Write the measures as the other.

176 ounces   29 pounds

Day 104
Review

Let's say that there were 1000 people there to watch Abraham's purchase and 6 were left. How many remained?

How many people would still be there if 183 were left from 1000?

Now let's say there are 598 people present and they are divided into 13 groups. If one of those groups left, how many people remained there?

87 x 53 =

Day 105
Review

What's ten percent of $6.10?

What percent of one dollar is $5.00?

$^8/_8$ x $^2/_9$ = $^2/_9$ x $^4/_5$ =

840 ($^3/_{24}$) =   126 ($^4/_7$) =

Day 106

Draw a circle to be the flock all together. Divide it into four parts. Color in three parts. Let's say that part of the flock had been watered. What part of the flock is still thirsty?

Write the fraction that shows what part of the flock had gotten a drink.

Which is bigger? Use < or > to show it.

How much of the flock is represented by those who have had a drink and those who haven't?

Draw seven circles. Let's say those represent seven sheep before Jacob watered them. How many had a drink so far?

What fractions could you add together to get to one?

Let's start with the whole flock and subtract off those who have had their drink. How many haven't if two fifths have?

What about if five sixths have?

What about if five twelfths have?

What about if seven ninths have?

What if three more times had been watered than not? Then how many would have had a drink if two ninths of the flock hadn't?

Draw a picture to show six ninths. Figure out an equivalent fraction with a smaller denominator.

Do it again with four fifteenths.

Do it again with five eighteenths.

Day 107

What time is it?

I'm going to tell you two times. One is when Leah was snuck into Jacob's tent. One is when he found out he had been tricked. You are going to draw the times on the clocks and then figure out how much time has elapsed, how long it took them to get there.

Leah snuck in at ten at night and Jacob found out at five in the afternoon.

Try it with these times: 11:00 AM and 3:00 PM.

Elapsed time: Elapsed time:

Count by fives to figure out how many minutes that is.

What time does the first clock say?   What time is it on the second clock?

Now draw these times and figure how long it took Jacob to learn he had been tricked. Leah snuck into his tent at ten thirty at night and Jacob found out at six in the morning.

Find the elapsed time with these times: 12:15 PM and 3:30 PM.

Elapsed time: Elapsed time:

Draw these times and figure how long it took Jacob to figure out he had been tricked.
seven twenty at night and four forty-five that following morning
9:05 AM and 3:27 PM

Elapsed time: Elapsed time:

Draw these times and figure how long it took Jacob to figure out he had been tricked.
ten thirty-four at night and two twelve the following morning
12:49 PM and 3:14 PM the next day

Elapsed time: Elapsed time:

Day 108

What's three four times?   What's three times six?

Count by fives with tally marks to figure out five times five and five times seven. Use tally marks to ten to figure out what is one half times ten.

What's one half times eight?   What's one half times twelve?   What's 20 times ½?

10 x 1 =   10 x 0 =   10 x 10 =

340 x 25 =

570 x 42 =

680 x 91 =

123 x 45 =

379 x 26 =

718 x 32 =

Day 109

If two sons were born and one was born to Leah, what fraction of the sons were born to Leah? Draw two people. Circle one of them. Write the fraction showing how many were Leah's sons.

Add two more sons to your drawing and circle two more. Write the new fraction.

If three fifths were Leah's sons and then two fifths were her maid's sons, how many of the sons were "from" Leah? Write the equation with the answer.

Write another fractional equation that equals one.

If Jacob had seven sons and three were Leah's, write an equation with the answer to show what fraction of the group that were not hers.

Write another fraction subtraction equation.

If three times more sons were from Leah than were not, how many were not from Leah if 12 sons were Leah's? Answer the question and then write it as a fraction. Reduce the fraction.

Do it again. If four times more sons were from Leah than were not, how many were not from Leah if 20 were from Leah? Answer the question and then write it as a fraction.

Day 110
Review

What if four more times sheep had had a drink than had not? Then how many would have had a drink if two twelfths of the flock hadn't? Reduce the fraction.

If four times the number of sons were Leah's as were not, how many were not if 28 were Leah's? Answer the question and then write it as a fraction.

Draw these times and figure how long it took Jacob to realize he had been tricked.
six fourteen in the evening and seven in the morning

2:39 AM and 4:04 PM the next day (doesn't quite make sense, but go with it)

Elapsed time: Elapsed time:

493 x 52 =

Day 111

If the servant was given five talents and returned with double, how many talents did he have in the end?

If the servant was given twelve talents and came back with double, how many talents did he have in the end?

If the servant was given forty-three talents and got back double, how many talents did he have in the end?

Let's say the servant was given eight talents and, in the end, just had five when he returned. What happened?   8 talents _____ = 5 talents

If the servant ended up with twenty-four talents and had started with seven, how many talents did he earn along the way?

If the servant ended up with one hundred thirteen talents and had started with seventy-six, how many talents did he earn?

If the servant ended up with two hundred twenty-two talents and had started with one hundred five, how many talents did he earn?

If the servant started with ten talents and ended with four talents, how many talents did he "earn?"

If the servant earned five times the amount he was given, how much did he earn if he had been given 27 talents?

If the servant earned twenty-four times the amount he was given, how much did he earn if he had been given 39 talents?

If the servant earned eight times the amount he was given, how much did he earn if he had been given 356 talents?

If the servant started with one hundred talents and ended with forty-six talents, how many talents did he "earn?"

If the servant earned a fifth of what he was given, how much did he earn if he was originally given 275 talents?

If the servant earned a sixteenth of what he was given, how much did he earn if he was originally given 224 talents?

If the servant earned a seventh of what he was given, how much did he earn if he was originally given 217 talents?

If the servant started with one thousand five hundred talents and ended with seven hundred sixty-eight talents, how many talents did he "earn?"

Day 112

One liter is 1000 milliliters. How many milliliters is two liters of oil?

How many liters of oil is 5000 milliliters of oil?

How many milliliters is half a liter?

Cut out the pieces in your workbook and figure out the following:

How many cups are in a pint?   How many pints are in one quart?

How many quarts are in a gallon?

Use what you know. How many pints are in a gallon?

How many cups are in a quart?

How many cups are in a gallon?

Use what you know. What part of a gallon is a cup?   A pint?   A quart?

What part of a quart is a pint?

Can you write that as a decimal?   Can you write that as a percent?

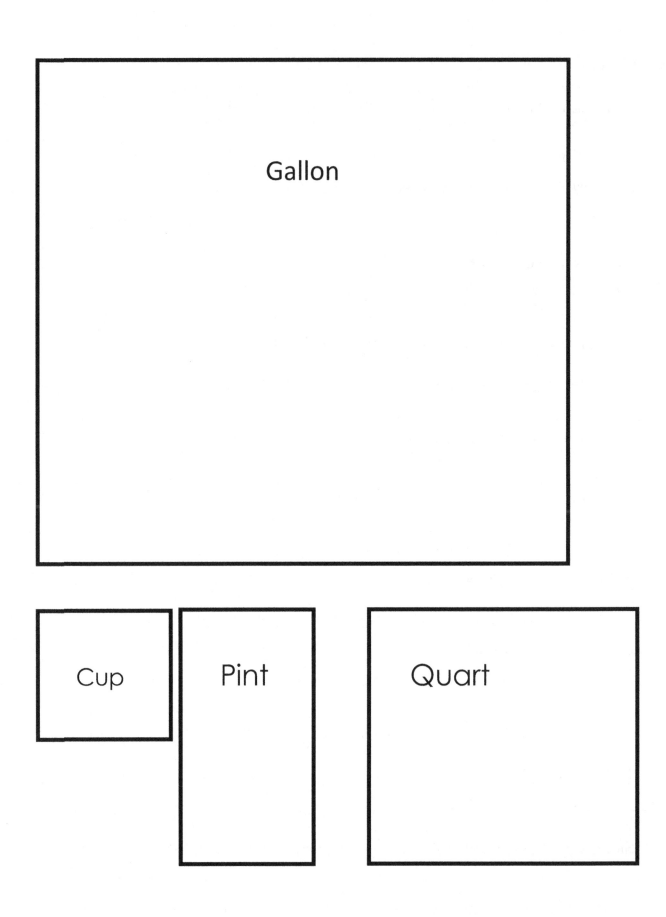

Day 113

The capital letter I represents the number 1. What number do you think is III?

The capital letter V represents the number 5. What number do you think is VI?

The capital letter X represents the number 10. What number do you think is XV?

Figure out what these numbers are:

VII =   XVI =   II =   XIII =

If VI is 6, what do you think is IV?

XVI is ten, five, one or sixteen. What's XIV?

Figure out these numbers:

XX =   IX =   XIX =   XIV =

Let's learn more letters. L = 50 and C = 100 What would be XL?

How would you write 300?

How would you write:

150 =   190 =   340 =   280 =

Learn two more letters. D = 500 and M = 1000 What would be 1984 in Roman numerals?

How would you write these numbers?

2017   570   499   1238

Day 114

We're going to read and write Roman Numerals today again. Do you remember how to write 1, 5, or 10?

How do you think you would write 15?

Figure out what these numbers are:

VIII =   XX =   XVII =   XI =

XI is eleven. What's IX?

Figure out these numbers:

IX =   XXIV =   XIII =   XXXVI =

Do you remember what letters represent 50 and 100?

How would you write 253?

How would you write:

175 =   196 =   284 =

Do you remember how to write 500 and 1000?

What would be 1769 in Roman numerals?

How would you write these numbers?

1092 =   484 =   999 =   3149 =

Day 115
Review

There are sixteen cups in a gallon. What fraction shows how many cups in a half gallon? What fraction of a half-gallon is one cup?

There are two cups in a pint. What percentage of a pint is a cup?

If the servant gave to Rebekah a sixth of what he was given, how much did he give her if he was originally given 318 talents?

If the servant started with two thousand three hundred talents and ended with one thousand one hundred twenty-six talents, how many talents did he "earn?"

Find 1, 5, 10, 15, 20, and 25 percent of $27.00.

$27.00 →

How would you write these numbers in Roman numerals?

1931   2759

Day 116

Write an amount of money with a bunch of zeros. Make sure to use a dollar sign and decimal point.

Now double that amount.   Now double that amount.   Now double that amount.

Here's a subtraction example.

	$3.15	315
	- $1.20	- 120
	2.00	200
	-.10	-10
	+.05	5
	$1.95	195 -> $1.95

Let's say the tunic is usually priced $42.95, but today it's on sale for just $15.80. How much could you save if you bought it today?

You buy the tunic for $42.95 and thread for $3.76. How much did you spend?

Let's say the tunic is usually priced $62.05, but today it's on sale for just $23.80. How much could you save if you bought it today?

You buy the tunic for $78.50 and a yarn for $4.67. How much did you spend?

Let's say the tunic is ten times more expensive than the cloak that costs $35.17. How much does the tunic cost?

What do you think is $35.17 times ten if 3517 times ten is 35,170?

Now multiply $35.17 by 100. First think, what's 3517 times 100?

Multiply these amounts by ten and one hundred:

$2.05

$14.67

$243.99

How do you think you could multiply 0.5 by ten?   How do you think you would divide 7 by ten?

Multiply and divide by ten over and over. Place your answer on the next line.

10 x 13.452 =
10 x
10 x
10 x
10 x

134.52   ÷ 10 =
          ÷ 10 =
          ÷ 10 =
          ÷ 10 =
          ÷ 10 =

Day 117

You are going to draw a map. Mark one place on the page, "You are here." Mark another place on the page as where the brothers and flock were.

Draw streets to get from here to there.

Decide how far each centimeter or inch on your drawing is in miles or kilometers.

Measure the distance along the roads Joseph would need to travel to get to the brothers and the flock.

Multiply that amount by the distance represented by each measurement.

How far would Joseph need to travel to get there?

Day 118

If you sold six bags of cookies to each of three customers, how many bags of cookies did you sell all together?

What if you sold three bags of cookies to each of six customers, how many bags would you have sold all together?

What if you received two votes from three different families for best snowman, how many votes did you receive all together?

If you sold twelve bags of cookies to each of three customers, how many bags of cookies did you sell all together?

What if you received twenty-one votes from three different families for best snowman, how many votes did you receive all together?

If you sold twelve bags of cookies in total to three people, how many bags of cookies did you sell to each person if they each bought the same number of bags?

If you sold twenty bags of cookies in total to four people, how many bags of cookies did you sell to each person if they each bought the same number of bags?

Let's say you got forty votes from ten families. Divide to find out about how many people voted from each family.

If you sold sixty-four bags of cookies to each of three customers, how many bags of cookies did you sell all together?

What if you received twenty-seven votes from three different families for best snowman, how many votes did you receive all together?

If you sold three bags of cookies to each of one hundred fifty-eight customers, how many bags of cookies did you sell?

What if you received three votes from two hundred thirty-six voters for best snowman (for most creative, best design, highest quality construction), how many votes did you receive?

If you divided two hundred seven cookies into bags of nine cookies each, how many bags of cookies could you make?

If you divided three hundred seventy-eight cookies evenly into bags of fourteen cookies each, how many bags did you need?

If you divided one hundred twenty-three cookies into bags of six cookies each, how many cookies are left over without a bag?

If you divided two hundred seventy-nine cookies into bags of fifteen cookies each, how many cookies are left over without a bag?

Day 119

Now draw these times and figure how long Joseph was in the pit. They threw him in at ten in the morning and got him out at ten thirty. They threw him in at 11:00 PM and got him out at 11:30 PM.

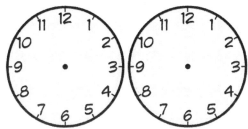 

Elapsed time: _____   Elapsed time: _____

They threw him in at nine in the morning and got him out at ten thirty-five.
Then let's say they threw him in at 11:15 AM and got him out at 11:40 AM.

Elapsed time: _____   Elapsed time: _____

They threw him in at eight twenty at night and got him out at ten forty. Then let's say they threw him in at 10:55 AM and pulled him out at 11:25 AM.

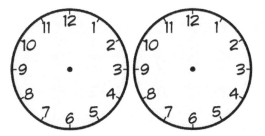 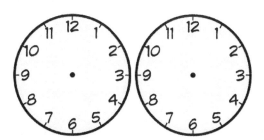

Elapsed time: _____   Elapsed time: _____

They threw him in at nine twenty-four in the morning and got him out at eleven twelve. Then let's say they threw him in at 11:43 AM and left him there until 7:27 PM.

Elapsed time: Elapsed time:

Day 120
Review

10 x 21.379 =

10 x   10 x

10 x   10 x

527.84   ÷ 10 =

                ÷ 10 =   ÷ 10 =

                ÷ 10 =   ÷ 10 =

Draw a line that's six centimeters long and write how far that would be if it were on a map where each centimeter represented 150 miles.

If you divided six hundred and twelve cookies evenly into bags of seventeen cookies each, how many bags did you need?

If you sold twenty-eight bags of cookies to each of thirty-six customers, how many bags of cookies did you sell?

Draw these times and figure how long Joseph was in the pit. They threw him in at 9:31 AM and let him there until 5:12 PM.

Elapsed time:

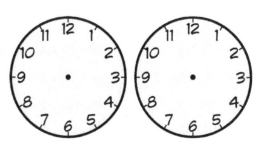

Day 121

If the house were five yards long and ten yards wide, what would its area be?

What would you need to know to find the surface area of the whole room, the total area of all the surfaces you want to paint?

Let's say there was a room that was the shape of a perfect cube. What would that look like? How many sides would it have?

In a perfect cube each of the six sides is a square. If each side had an area of 5 meters squared, what would be the total surface area of the cube?

Find the surface area of a cube where each side is a square with a length of ten centimeters.

What would be the surface area of a cube where each side had a length of five inches?

What would be the surface area of a cube where each side had a length of twenty-three centimeters?

What would be the surface area of a cube where each side had a length of eighteen inches?

What would be the surface area of a cube where each side had a length of twenty-five centimeters?

What would be the surface area of a cube where each side had a length of sixty-eight inches?

If the surface area of a cube were 384 in², what is the length of one side?

If the surface area of a cube were 726 cm², what is the length of one side?

Day 122

Roll a die over and over again and jot down a tally mark in each column when that number comes up. Do it about thirty times.

Flip a coin twenty times. Record what side it lands on each time. What is the outcome? What should be the outcome?

What's the chance of a head coming up? You can write that as a fraction. $^1/_2$

If there was one red, one blue, and one yellow marble in a bowl, and you picked one out, what are the chances you picked out the blue one?

There are two red marbles, three blue marbles, one yellow marble, four green marbles, and five white marbles in a bowl. What is the probability of each color being chosen at random? Write the answers as fractions. Can you reduce any of those fractions to make equivalent fractions with smaller denominators?

red: yellow:

blue: green:

white:

Day 123

If you were given $100 three times, how much would you have? What if you were given $120 dollars three times? What if you were given $123 dollars three times?

If you were given $1000 three times, how much would you have?

If you were given $1400 three times, how much would you have?

If you were given $1430 three times, how much would you have?

If you were given $1436 three times, how much would you have?

If you were given $674 three times, how much would you have?

If you were given $49 thirty-three times, how much would you have?

If you were given $693 by someone giving you three gifts of the same amount, how much did they give you each time?

If you were given $452 by someone giving you three gifts of almost the same amount except the last one had just a little more in it, how much did they give you each time and how much extra was in the last amount?

If you were given $197 by someone giving you three gifts of almost the same amount except the last one had just a little more in it, how much did they give you each time and how much extra was in the last amount?

Day 124

If one piece of silver was worth $4.23, how much would two pieces be worth?

$4.23
+ $4.23

If one piece of silver was worth $32.14, how much would two pieces be worth?

If one piece of silver was worth $0.50, how much would two pieces be worth?

If one piece of silver was worth $1.50, how much would two pieces be worth?

If one piece of silver was worth $10.50, how much would two pieces be worth?

If one piece of silver was worth $6.47, how much would two pieces be worth?

If one piece of silver was worth $23.61, how much would two pieces be worth?

If one piece of silver was worth $40.75, how much would two pieces be worth?

If one piece of silver was worth $46.99, how much would two pieces be worth?

If one piece of silver was worth $128.27, how much would two pieces be worth?

If one piece of silver was worth $135.90, how much would two pieces be worth?

If one piece of silver was worth $281.50, how much would two pieces be worth?

If one piece of silver was worth $890.67, how much would two pieces be worth?

If one piece of silver was worth $567.89, how much would two pieces be worth?

If one piece of silver was worth $2671.53, how much would two pieces be worth?

If one piece of silver was worth $9999.99, how much would two pieces be worth?

Day 125
Review

If the surface area of a cube were 3750 cm², what is the length of one side?

There are two yellow marbles, three red marbles, one blue marble, four white marbles, and five green marbles in a bowl. What is the probability of each color being chosen at random? Write the answers as fractions. Can you reduce any of those fractions to make equivalent fractions with smaller denominators?

If you were given $347 by someone giving you three gifts of almost the same amount except the last one had just a little more in it, how much did they give you each time and how much extra was in the last amount

If one piece of silver was worth $3948.75, how much would two pieces be worth?

Day 126

Write one third and two thirds as fractions.

If there had been ten baskets and the birds had eaten out of half of them, how many would that be?

Draw ten baskets. Probably best to just draw ten circles. Put an X in three of them and write the fraction and decimal shown by the picture. Put an X in one more and write that fraction. Do the same thing two more times.

Draw a box and divide into four parts.

Add together the four fractions you wrote in the previous section.

What mixed number does eighteen tenths equal?

Each of the fractions below is an equivalent fraction to either three tenths, four tenths, five tenths, or six tenths. An equivalent fraction is an equal fraction, like $1/2 = 2/4$. You can draw a picture of a box and divide into four parts and then color in half of it to show that it is true. Write the equivalent fraction of each of these fractions.

$6/20 =$ $3/5 =$ $1/2 =$ $9/30 =$

Bonus: Reduce eight tenths. Make the numerator and denominator smaller.

Each of these fractions is an equivalent fraction to either three tenths, four tenths, five tenths, or six tenths. Write the equivalent fraction of each of these fractions.

$2/5 =$ $36/60 =$ $20/40 =$ $6/15 =$

Now find another equivalent fraction for each of them. Reduce each fraction as far as you can.

$2/5$ $3/5$ $1/2$ $2/5$

Now add together all of these new equivalent fractions (two fifths, etc.)

Add this mixed number with your previous answer of one and eight tenths. Reduce the fraction if possible.

Day 127

Write one ninth as a fraction.

If two fifths of the dream was about the cows and then three fifths of the dream was about the ears of grain, how much of the dream would that have been?

If the cow part of the dream was two sevenths of it and then the grain part was four sevenths of the dream, how much of the dream was that?

If the cow part of the dream was one ninth of the dream and then the ear part was four ninths of the dream, how much of the dream was that?

Try it with three eighths and four eighths.

Write the equation and answer with mixed numbers. If three and two thirds of his dreams were about the cows and ears and one and one third was about the ears of grain, how much of his dreams were about the cows?

Try it with fourteen and three fifths with eight and one fifth.

Try it with thirty and seven ninths with sixteen and two ninths.

Try it with twelve fifths and six fifths. Write the equation and answer with improper fractions (where the numerator is bigger than the denominator) and then again with mixed numbers.

If three fifths of his dreams were about cows and he had dreams about ears of grain four times that many times, how much of his dreams were about ears of grain? Write the answer as an improper fraction and as a mixed number.

Try it with: seven twelfths fourteen times
Write the answer as an improper fraction and as a mixed number. Reduce the fraction in the mixed number if it is possible.

If both numbers are even, you can always divide them both by two to reduce the fraction and find an equivalent fraction. Remember that all of those answers are equal amounts.

Try it with: nine fifths seventeen times Write the answer as an improper fraction and as a mixed number. Reduce the fraction in the mixed number if it is possible.

How do you think you would multiply $3\,^5/_6$ by eight?

Can you divide 4 and 6 each by the same number to reduce the fraction and get an equivalent fraction?

Day 128

Draw a picture that shows one half.

Write out those fifths you just answered, from one fifth to five fifths.

Add together the fractions you just wrote.

If you had fifteen fingers, how many hands would you have?

Draw five circles. Color in one of them. Color in half of each of the other circles. Add together the colored parts. How much do you have? Write the equation and the answer. 1 + ½ + … =

If you had four and a half circles colored in and then erased one and a half of them, how many would be colored in?

Subtract forty and seven eighths minus twelve and three eighths.

Find the equivalent fraction of the fraction with the smaller denominator that has the same denominator as the other fraction. Then find the answer.

$^2/_6$ + $^2/_3$ =

$^4/_{15}$ + $^2/_5$ =

$^2/_3$ - $^1/_6$ =

$^4/_6$ - $^1/_3$ =

Think! How would you subtract $7\ ^1/_4$ - $4\ ^5/_8$?

Here's one more to try. $8\ ^1/_3$ - $3\ ^4/_6$

Day 129

What fraction describes one of the two pieces of Egypt if it were divided in half?

Draw a picture that shows six out of seven things, six sevenths, $6/7$. Draw a picture that shows three out of four parts of one whole object, three fourths, $3/4$.

Add one and one fourth plus three and two fourths. Add twenty-five and one fifth plus seventeen and three fifths.

If Egypt were divided in two, and one part was $1/8$ of the whole land, what fraction shows the size of the other part? If Egypt was in two parts, and one part was $3/14$ of the whole of Egypt, what fraction shows the size of the other part?

Find the difference between one hundred and seven fifteenths and thirty-four and two fifteenths.

Find the difference between fifty-two and eight fifteenths and seven and three fifteenths.

Find the sum of seven twelfths and eight twelfths. Write your answer as an improper fraction and then as a mixed number. Then reduce the fractional part of the mixed number.

Multiply four fifths times six sevenths.   Multiply four sixths times five eighths.

Multiply five halves by six ninths.

Day 130
Review

Fill in the blank in the equivalent fractions.

$2/5 = ?/10$ $36/60 = ?/10$ $20/40 = 5/?$

Multiply seven fifteenths and nineteen. Write the answer as an improper fraction and as a mixed number. Reduce the fraction in the mixed number if it is possible.

Multiply $5\,4/9$ by three.

$7\,1/3 - 3\,4/9 =$

Multiply seven halves by eight ninths.

Day 131

What if three more times sheep had been watered than not? Then how many would have been watered if two twelfths hadn't? Reduce the fraction.

Draw these times and figure how long it took them to reach the mountains. They started at six fourteen in the morning and got there at one seven that afternoon. Try it with these times: 2:39 AM and got there at 4:04 PM the next day.

573 x 250 =

Day 132

There are sixteen cups in a gallon. What fraction shows one cup out of a half gallon?

28 x 36 =

Identify how many sets of parallel lines are in the shapes.

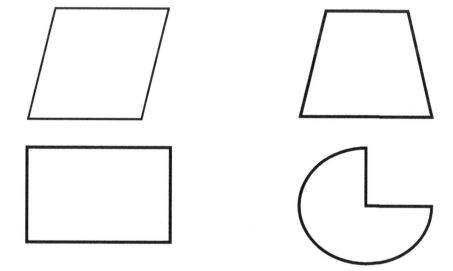

Day 133

$7 \frac{2}{3} - 3 \frac{4}{9} =$

Multiply seven halves by eight ninths.

Draw a line that's ten centimeters long. What distance would that mean on a map where each centimeter represented 150 miles?

If you divided six hundred and twelve cookies evenly into bags of seventeen cookies each, how many bags did you make?

$49 \times 68 =$

Day 134

If seven fifteenths of Pharaoh's dreams were about cows and he dream about grain nineteen times as often, how much of Pharaoh's dreams were about grain? Write the answer as an improper fraction and as a mixed number. Reduce the fraction in the mixed number if it is possible.

Multiply $5 \, {}^4/_9$ by three.

Find 32% of $15.

How would you write these numbers in Roman Numerals?

1931, 2759

279 x 470 =

Day 135

319.26 $\div$ 10 =

            $\div$ 10 =

            $\div$ 10 =

            $\div$ 10 =

            $\div$ 10 =

2210 $\div$ 65 =

1234 x 5 =

Day 136

If one piece of silver was worth $3948.25, how much would two piece be worth?

$2/5 = ?/10$ $36/60 = ?/10$ $20/40 = 5/?$

If a slave started with two thousand three hundred talents and ended with one thousand one hundred twenty-six talents, how many talents did he "earn?"

Find 42% of $63.

5678 x 9 =

Day 137

There are two yellow marbles, three red marbles, one blue marble, four white marbles, and five green marbles in a bowl. What is the probability of each color being chosen at random? Write the answers as fractions. Can you reduce any of those fractions to make equivalent fractions with smaller denominators? (Hint: If both numbers are even, you can at least divide the top and bottom, the numerator and denominator by two.)

If you were given $347 by someone giving you three gifts of almost the same amount except the last one had just a little more in it, how much did they give you each time and how much extra was in the last amount (hint: the remainder)?

There are two cups in a pint. What percentage of a pint is a cup?

If the slave earned a sixth of his original investment, how much did he earn if he was originally given 318 talents?

372 x 480 =

Day 138

Draw these times and figure how much time elapsed. 9:31 PM and 5:12 AM

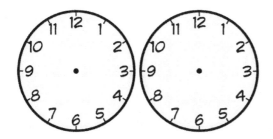

If the surface area of a cube were 3750 cm², what is the length of one side?

684 x 720 =

Day 139

Divide 612 into groups of 17.

If you sold twenty-eight bags of cookies to each of thirty-six customers, how many bags of cookies did you sell?

If four times the number of people left as remained, how many left if 28 remained? Answer the question and then write it as a fraction.

$10.00 $10.00 $10.00
- $5.27   - $2.81   - $9.64

Day 140

10 x 42.583 =

10 x

10 x

10 x

10 x

1652 ÷ 28 =

6398 x 7 =

Day 141

1596	7149	254	86,000
+ 4127	+ 2835	+ 348	+ 14,000

What time is it?

How many hours is 30 days?

If Abraham was 56 miles into a 207 mile trip, how much farther does He have to walk?

Day 142

755	2143	234	58,000
+ 482	+ 6275	+ 398	+ 42,000

What time does the clock say?

Find the sum: 170 + 103 + 256 + 369

How many dollars would you need to get to six hundred forty-three dollars if you had three hundred eighty-seven dollars of debt?

Day 143

```
  2169          782          976          3073
+ 4852        + 255        + 348        + 1848
```

Write fifty-six thousand two hundred fifty-nine on the chart.

ten thousands	thousands	hundreds	tens	ones

Write this number in expanded form: 32,179.

How many pieces of fruit were in the orchard if it had 64 trees and there were 82 pieces of fruit on each tree?

Day 144

7259	586	2905	3674
+ 8464	+ 835	+ 3418	+ 3475

Find the sum: 422 + 260 + 325

Multiply: 531 x 800

What would the area be of a rectangle width of 7 and a length of 34?

Day 145

$56 \div 7 =$ $81 \div 9 =$ $64 \div 8 =$ $24 \div 3 =$

$42 \div 6 =$ $45 \div 9 =$ $36 \div 6 =$ $49 \div 7 =$

$$\begin{array}{r} 46 \\ \times\ 8 \\ \hline \end{array}$$ $$\begin{array}{r} 37 \\ \times\ 6 \\ \hline \end{array}$$ $$\begin{array}{r} 28 \\ \times\ 7 \\ \hline \end{array}$$ $$\begin{array}{r} 68 \\ \times\ 5 \\ \hline \end{array}$$

$$\begin{array}{r} 45 \\ \times\ 18 \\ \hline \end{array}$$ $$\begin{array}{r} 82 \\ \times\ 26 \\ \hline \end{array}$$ $$\begin{array}{r} 39 \\ \times\ 47 \\ \hline \end{array}$$ $$\begin{array}{r} 280 \\ \times\ 570 \\ \hline \end{array}$$

$1638 \div 21 =$

Day 146

6510	5400	3482	6300
- 4125	- 2350	- 2341	- 1441

If there were 324 people and 152 left the area, how many would be remaining?

If you owed $560 and paid back $7 a day, how long would it be before you paid off your debt?

½ + ¼ =

Day 147

6720	5436	5642	5000
- 4823	- 2751	- 3982	- 4200

What's double this number? 476

How many things would you have picked up if you picked up 178 things six times?

Find the sum: 4582 + 2060

Day 148

211	2820	426	3713
- 412	- 2556	- 348	- 1458

How many lines of symmetry does an oval have?

Find the difference between 6314 meters and 2058 meters.

How many grapes would there be if there 56 bunches and 14 grapes on each bunch?

Day 149

```
   464        5860        3654        3150
 - 251      - 2350      - 3485      - 3470
```

Multiply: 64 x 370

Find the sum: 689 + 129 + 387

What would the area be of a rectangle width of 15 centimeters and a length of 29 cm?

Day 150

63 ÷ 7 =   36 ÷ 9 =   56 ÷ 8 =   27 ÷ 3 =

24 ÷ 6 =   54 ÷ 9 =   42 ÷ 6 =   35 ÷ 7 =

$$\begin{array}{r} 45 \\ \times\ 6 \\ \hline \end{array}$$
$$\begin{array}{r} 37 \\ \times\ 8 \\ \hline \end{array}$$
$$\begin{array}{r} 24 \\ \times\ 7 \\ \hline \end{array}$$
$$\begin{array}{r} 89 \\ \times\ 4 \\ \hline \end{array}$$

$$\begin{array}{r} 37 \\ \times\ 28 \\ \hline \end{array}$$
$$\begin{array}{r} 41 \\ \times\ 76 \\ \hline \end{array}$$
$$\begin{array}{r} 58 \\ \times\ 55 \\ \hline \end{array}$$
$$\begin{array}{r} 29 \\ \times\ 97 \\ \hline \end{array}$$

1100 ÷ 19 =
Write the remainder if necessary.

Day 151

Draw a trapezoid on the graph. Make sure to include negative coordinates. Write its coordinates. Find its area.

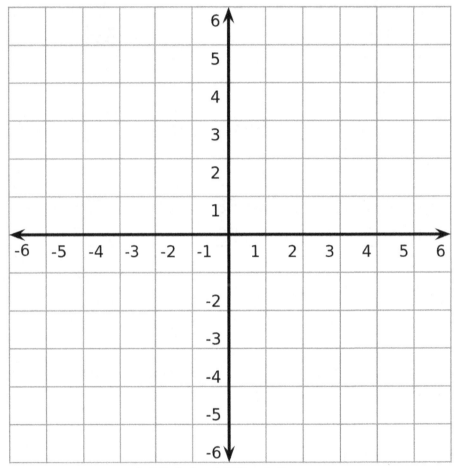

By H Padleckas via Wikimedia Commons

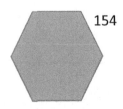 154

Find the perimeter.

Day 152

4719	$10.00	5185	$10.00
+ 684	- $1.97	+ 4836	- $7.83

Let's say you had seven dimes, three quarters, and thirteen nickels and wanted to buy the train toy for ninety-one cents. How much do you have left after you buy the train?

What's $3/8$ (72)?

Subtract one fifth from one. Write the equation and answer.

Day 153

```
  1586        $10.00        5185        $10.00
+  785      -  $5.30      + 3078      -  $4.87
```

What's $5/7$ (84)?

```
  245          587
x  61        x  43
```

Day 154

2417	$10.00	5395	$10.00
+ 690	- $2.70	+ 4878	- $3.16

Let's say there are six hundred seventy-one animals owned by Laban and Isaac had two hundred eighty-eight of them and seventy-five of them were sheep. How many of all the animals were not Isaac's sheep?

Find the missing number.

$$\_\_\_\_\_ \times 14 = 322 \qquad\qquad \_\_\_\_\_ \div 4 = 275$$

Day 155

2887	$10.00	395	$10.00
+ 1698	- $1.60	x 78	- $2.84

What's $\frac{4}{9}$ (243)?

Use a Groups and Totals chart to divide 429 by five. Write a reminder if necessary.

Day 156

Let's say that there are 27 flights of stairs and each flight has 19 steps in them. How many stairs are there all together?)

Round these numbers to the closest hundred.

350 →   149 →   850 →   978 →

What's $5/12$ (780)?   How many groups of 16 are in 538? Always write a reminder if necessary.

Day 157

Multiply seven hundred thousand by ten.

Divide seven million by ten.

Let's say that Abraham traveled 100 minutes before breakfast, 353 minutes between breakfast and lunch, and another 387 minutes after lunch. About how many hours did he travel that day? Estimate the answer by rounding to the nearest hundred, then rounding to the nearest ten, and then find the exact answer.

What's $9/14$ (364)?   How many groups of 23 are in 1100?

Day 158

Combine these numbers. - 371, 614, - 375, 246, - 119

Let's say Abraham stayed 168 days all together in 4 towns, the same amount of time in each city. How many days did He spend in each city? Estimate the answer by rounding to the nearest hundred, then rounding to the nearest ten, and then find the exact answer.

What's $5/12$ (780)?   How many groups of 16 are in 560?

Day 159

If one part of the garden had 24 trees with 76 fruits on it and another part had 34 trees that had 58 fruits, which has more fruit? Compare their number of crops using a greater than/less than symbol.

Let's say Abraham left at 5:50 in the morning and reached the mountain at 3:17 in the afternoon. How long was he traveling? Draw the times and find the elapsed time.

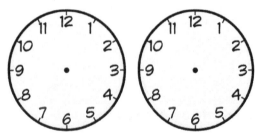   Elapsed time:

Day 160

8497	$10.00	826	$10.00
+ 543	- $4.16	x 18	- $5.72

What's $9/4$ (144)?

Use a Groups and Totals chart to divide 322 by seven.

Day 161

How would you write these numbers in Roman Numerals?

1953, 474

Measure two things in your house and write down their measurement in inches in fractions. You can use your page on Day 72 to help you.

451 x 38 =

Day 162

Write the value of a penny, a nickel, a dime, and a quarter as decimals.

Write as decimals 35 hundredths, 68 and 2 hundredths.

Now convert them to fractions.

392 x 64 =

Day 163

Write these numbers and then read them out loud.
millions , hundred thousand | ten thousand | thousand , hundreds | tens | ones

four hundred twenty-nine thousand, four hundred three

twelve million six hundred seventy-four thousand thirteen

Multiply.

394 x 76 =

Let's say you had four hundred fifty-six dollars of debt and got one thousand dollars. How much money would you have after you paid your debt?

Day 164

```
  5013          $21.78
- 2738         - $17.90
```

Write three and a third and one and one ninth each as a mixed number and an improper fraction. Add the improper fractions and add the mixed numbers. Convert the improper fraction into a mixed number. Do the answers match?

$1900 \div 26 =$

Day 165

Find the sum or difference. Then do the opposite to see if your answers make sense.

$$\begin{array}{r} \$5.00 \\ -\$2.74 \\ \hline \end{array} \qquad \begin{array}{r} \$9.65 \\ +\$0.78 \\ \hline \end{array} \qquad \begin{array}{r} \$10.00 \\ -\$4.61 \\ \hline \end{array}$$

Multiply $24.76 by five.

$3510 \div 20 =$

Day 166

478 x 36 =

Answer the question and the do the opposite to check the work.

468 ÷ 18 =

Day 167

Find your profit. Buy at $273.96, and sell at $500.00.

If the sacrifice weighed one twelfth of the altar, how much did it weigh if the altar weighed 4164 grams?

Draw a line that is 3.8 cm.

Multiply thirteen halves by seven ninths.

Day 168

If the moles living in the molehill weighed one fourteenth of the molehill, how much did they weigh if the molehill was 392 pounds?

A pound is sixteen ounces. An ounce is one sixteenth of a pound. Write the measures as the other.

208 ounces   35 pounds

Subtract and reduce.

$10 \, ^2/_3 - 5 \, ^5/_9 =$

Day 169

Let's say that there were 1000 people and 16 left. How many remained?

How many would remain if 257 left from 1000 that were there?

Now let's say there are 598 people and they are divided into 13 groups. If one of those groups left, how many people would still be there?

Multiply $16 \frac{8}{9}$ by eight.

Change the improper fraction in the answer into a mixed number. Combine it with 16 x 8 and then reduce the fraction if possible.

Day 170

What's ten percent of $7.30?

What percent of one dollar is $8.00?

$^8/_8$ x $^2/_9$ = $^2/_9$ x $^4/_5$ =

840 ($^3/_{24}$) =   126 ($^4/_7$) =

Day 171

What if four more times sheep had been watered than not? Then how many would have been watered if two twelfths of the flock hadn't? Reduce the fraction.

Draw these times and figure how long it took them to reach the mountains. They started at six fourteen in the morning and got there at one seven that afternoon. Try it with these times: 2:39 AM and got there at 4:04 PM the next day.

573 x 250 =

135 ÷ 6 =

Day 172

There are sixteen cups in a gallon. There are four cups in a quart. How many quarts are in a gallon?

287 x 560 =

Identify how many sets of parallel lines are in the shapes.

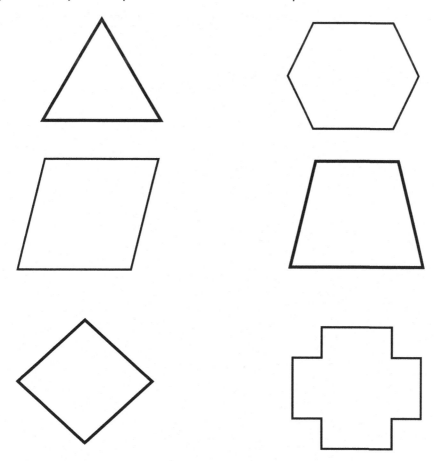

Day 173 (ruler)

$7 \frac{1}{3} - 3 \frac{4}{9} =$

Multiply seven halves by eight ninths. Write your answer as a mixed number. Draw a picture if that helps.

Draw a line that's four inches long. How far of a distance would that represent if it were on a map and each inch represented 400 miles?

If you divided six hundred twelve cookies evenly into bags of seventeen cookies each, how many cookies were in each bag?

$490 \times 687 =$

Day 174

If seven fifteenths of Pharaoh's dreams were about cows and he dream about grain nineteen times as often, how much of Pharaoh's dreams were about grain? Write the answer as an improper fraction and as a mixed number. Reduce the fraction in the mixed number if it is possible.

Multiply $5\,^4/_9$ by three.

Find 25% of $30.

How would you write these numbers in Roman Numerals?

940, 1465

$476 \div 17 =$

Day 175

319.26   ÷ 10 =

÷ 10 =

÷ 10 =

÷ 10 =

÷ 10 =

2210 ÷ 65 =

1234 x 5 =

Day 176

If one piece of silver was worth $1862.74, how much would two piece be worth?

$2/5 = ?/15$ $36/60 = ?/10$ $20/40 = 4/?$

If a slave started with two thousand three hundred talents and ended with one thousand one hundred twenty-six talents, how many talents did he "earn?"

Find 39% of $20.

$416 \div 8 =$

Day 177

There are two yellow marbles, three red marbles, and five green marbles in a bowl. What is the probability of each color being chosen at random? Write the answers as fractions. Can you reduce any of those fractions to make equivalent fractions with smaller denominators? (Hint: If both numbers are even, you can at least divide the top and bottom, the numerator and denominator by two.)

If you were given $374 by someone giving you three gifts of almost the same amount except the last one had just a little more in it, how much did they give you each time and how much extra was in the last amount (hint: the remainder)?

There are two cups in a pint. What percentage of a pint is a cup?

If the slave earned a sixth of his original investment, how much did he earn if he was originally given 318 talents?

372 x 480 =

Day 178

Draw these times and figure out how much time elapsed. 9:31 PM and 5:12 AM

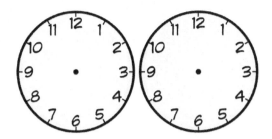

If the surface area of a cube were 2400 cm², what is the length of one side?

684 x 720 =

Day 179

Divide 615 into groups of 17.

If you sold seventeen bags of cookies to each of forty-nine customers, how many bags of cookies did you sell?

If four times the number of people left as remained, how many were stayed behind if 28 left? Answer the question and then write it as a fraction.

$10.00 $10.00 $10.00
- $5.27   - $2.81   - $9.64

Day 180

10 x 42.583 =

10 x

10 x

10 x

10 x

1655 ÷ 28 =

6398 x 7 =

Thank you for using the Genesis Curriculum.
Hope you had a great year of learning together.

Look for more years of the Genesis Curriculum using both Old and New Testament
books of the Bible. Find us online at genesiscurriculum.com to read about the latest
developments in this expanding curriculum.

GC Steps are three years of preschool and kindergarten that prepare students in reading,
writing, and math. These are aimed at children ages three to six.

Facts practice workbooks allow students to improve on their score each day using the
same timed practice sheet daily.

The Genesis Curriculum Rainbow Readers take quality reading and present them in a
new way. Each book stands alone and has a dictionary with the included vocabulary
underlined in the text. The books have also been edited to use modern American
spelling to help your children spell by knowing what looks right. Some of the books
have been lightly edited for content issues. There are also occasional helps with
explanations or pictures. They were made with GC students in mind.

GenesisCurriculum.com

Made in the USA
Columbia, SC
21 July 2020